HAMPI RUINS

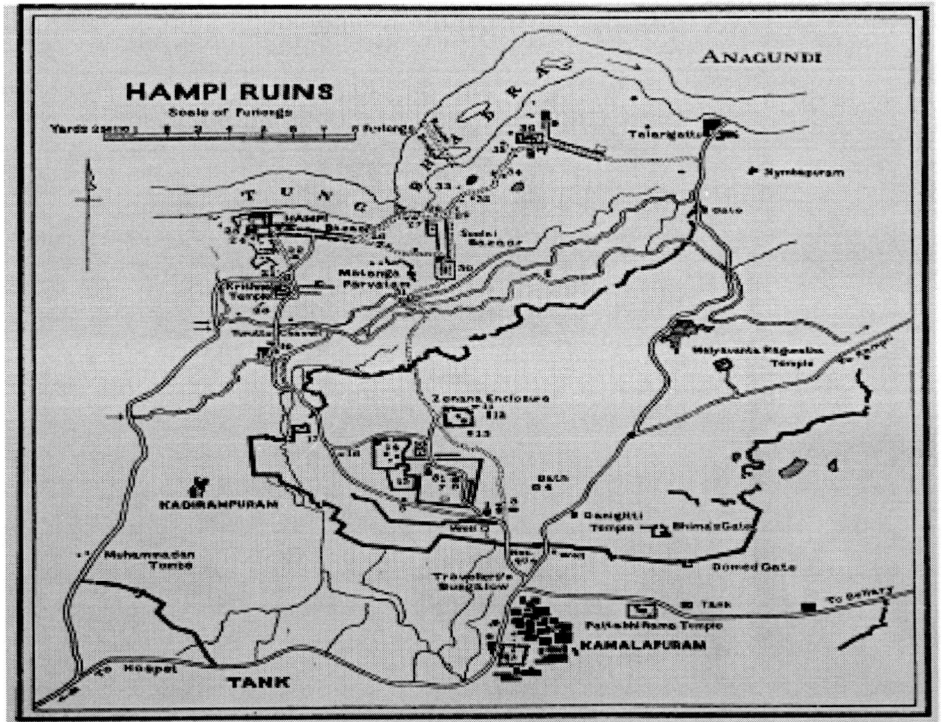

Reg. No. 2209

Helio-Zinco., Survey Office, Madras.

REFERENCES

1 Queen's Bath
2 Water Tower
3 Chandrasekhara Temple
4 Octagonal Bath
5 Octagonal Water Pavilion
6 Throne Platform
7 King's Palace
8 Underground Chamber
9 King's Audience Hall
10 Hazara Rāma Temple
11 Guard's Quarters
12 Elephant's Stables
13 Ranga Temple
14 Danaik's Enclosure
15 Mint
16 Underground Temple
17 Natural Archway
18 Sati Memorials
19 [illegible] Temple
20 Narasimha Statue
21 Sasivekalu Ganesa Shrine
22 Kadalaikalu Ganesa Temple
23 Hemakutam
24 Group of Jaina Temples
25 Pampapati Temple
26 Monolithic Bull
27 Kodanda Rāma Temple
28 Varaha Temple
29 Anantasayanam Temple
30 Achyuta Rāya's Temple
31 Steps leading up Matanga Parvatam
32 Jaina Temple
33 Sugriva's Cave
34 King's Balance
35 Unfinished Gateway
36 Vitthala Temple

HAMPI RUINS

DESCRIBED AND ILLUSTRATED

BY

A. H. LONGHURST

GYAN

Published by

Gyan Publishing House
5, Ansari Road
Daryaganj, New Delhi-110002
Phone: 011-47034999, 9811692060
E-mail: books@gyanbooks.com

Distribution Network
gyanbooks.com
India, USA, Canada, UK, Australia, France

ISBN : 978-81-212-3457-3 (PB)
First Published, Madras, 1917

2nd Impression 2020

Printed at: Gyan Press, Delhi.

Hampi Ruins
Author: A. H. Longhurst

HAMPI RUINS

DESCRIBED AND ILLUSTRATED

BY

A. H. LONGHURST,

Superintendent, Archæological Survey Department, Southern Circle

MADRAS

PRINTED BY THE SUPERINTENDENT, GOVERNMENT PRESS

1917

PREFACE

THE object of this little book is, not only to give a clear and brief description of the various styles of buildings produced during the Vijayanagar period, but also to consider those influences which have contributed to the formation of each special style. It is a mistake to isolate architecture from its surroundings, because the main points of the physical geography, social progress and historical development of any country require to be understood by those who would study and comprehend its particular style.

The leading influences that may be expected to shape the architecture of any country or people are—(1) Locality with regard to its geographical, geological, and climatic conditions; (2) Religion; (3) Social and Political; (4) Historical. Important as all four of these are, the strongest is undoubtedly the influence of religion. In almost all countries and in India in particular, we find that the chief buildings are the outcome of the nation's religious beliefs. Nothing reveals the character of the nation so clearly as its religion, and nothing has more permeating influence upon its architecture. Therefore, the influence of religion has been dealt with rather more fully than would at first sight perhaps appear necessary in a small work of this kind, but the necessity, however, for a brief knowledge of this important subject will become apparent when the visitor to Hampi finds himself confronted with the profusely sculptured walls and pillars adorning some of the larger temples. To him who knows not the legends of Rāma and Krishna, the different incarnations of Vishnu or the characteristics and attributes of Śiva, these wonderful 'pictures in stone' will have no meaning.

Time spent in the study of the architecture and religion of the past will never be regretted, for every ruin tells of the history of other days, and enables the character and conditions of men of past periods to be conjured up, thus opening wide to all students and lovers of old buildings the enjoyment of contemplating forms which will then have for them a meaning and a charm.

Part I deals with the main influences which have helped to form the different styles of architecture produced during the Vijayanagar period, and *Part II* describes the chief buildings existing at Hampi. *Part I* has been compiled mainly from the following works, and lays no claim to originality—Mr. Robert Sewell's book "A Forgotten Empire"* (a work that every visitor to Hampi should read); "The Bellary District Gazetteer"; "Mysore and Coorg, from the Inscriptions" by Mr. Lewis Rice; "Hinduism" by Mr. L. D. Barnett; and I am greatly indebted to Mr. Krishna Sastri, the Assistant Archæological Superintendent for Epigraphy to the Government of Madras, for assisting me with regard to the dates of the different rulers of Vijayanagar and much other valuable information.

In *Part II*, long descriptions which are necessarily technical and intolerably dry have been omitted. I have therefore provided the largest possible number of illustrations instead, and have confined the text to brief, but it is hoped vivid notes on the special qualities and characteristics of the buildings referred to.

The illustrations are from full-plate negatives in this office, and as per the orders of Government contained in G.O. No. 687, Public, dated the 9th April 1916, bromide or P.O.P. prints from any of these are available to the public at a cost of 8 annas each, postage paid, obtainable at the address mentioned below.

ARCH. SUR. DEPT., S. CIRCLE,
MADRAS, *November* 1916. A. H. LONGHURST.

---

* Published by Swan Sonnenschein & Co., London.

CONTENTS.

PART I.

INFLUENCES.

PART II.

THE BUILDINGS DESCRIBED.

LIST OF ILLUSTRATIONS.

Fig. 1.—Hampi Ruins from Hēmakutam Hill.

HAMPI RUINS.

PART I.

INFLUENCES.

LOCALITY.

Hampi is a tiny hamlet which grew up around the great Pampāpati temple which stands on the southern bank of the Tungabhadra in the Hospet taluk of the Bellary district of the Madras Presidency. It is of no importance in itself, but it has given its name to the ruins which lie scattered about it of Vijayanagar, "the City of Victory," the birth-place of the empire of that name and also of old the capital of its kings. Hampi.

The remains cover some nine square miles, but the fortifications and outposts of the city included a far larger area [see Fig. 1]. The entrance to it from the south-west, for instance, was at one time a fortified gateway on the huge embankment which stands at the foot of the hills two miles the other side of Hospet—nine miles as the crow flies from the centre of the ruins. The town of Ānegundi in the Nizam's Dominions formed the outpost for the city on its northern side, while Kampli served as an outpost on the eastern side.

The site of the old city is a strangely wild place to have been the birth-place and capital of an empire. The whole of it is dotted with little, barren, rocky hills and immediately north of it the wide and rapid Tungabhadra hurries along a boulder-strewn channel down rapids and through narrow gorges. The hills are of granite weathered to every shade of colour from grey to brown, and have hardly any vegetation on them. The alternate burning days and chilly nights of the Deccan climate have seamed and split in every direction the huge masses of solid rock of which they originally consisted, and the earthquakes of remote ages and the slower processes of denudation have torn from their flanks the enormous boulders which were thus formed and have piled

FIG. 2.—GROUP OF BOULDERS ON MALYAVANTA HILL.

these up round about their sides in the most fantastic confusion or flung them headlong into the valleys below. In places, cyclopean masses stand delicately poised one upon another at the most hazardous angles [see Fig. 2], in others they form impassable barriers, while those which have yet to fall often stand boldly out from the hills as single giant tors or range themselves in castellations and embattlements which but for their vastness would seem to be the work of man rather than of nature. A very remarkable formation of a natural archway is shown in Fig. 3. This is situated on the west side of the main road to Hampi close to the so-called Underground Temple and to the north of the latter.

The unlimited supply of splendid building material close at hand, had a considerable influence on the architecture of the city by rendering it possible, to acquire on the spot, huge blocks of stone of vast dimensions which otherwise would not have been so freely used owing to the difficulty of transporting them from a distance.

Up the sides of these hills and along the low ground between them—often in several lines one behind the other—run the fortified enclosing walls of the old city, and in the valleys among them stand its deserted streets and ruined temples and palaces. The lowest ground of all is covered with fields of tall cholam, sugarcane, or of green and golden rice watered by the channel which one of the kings of the days gone by led from the Tungabhadra to supply the people, and irrigate the orchards and rose-gardens, of his capital. To know Vijayanagar at its best, the visitor should climb the slippery steps leading to the little shrine on the top of the hill called Matanga Parvatam and watch the evening light fade across the ruins, and if the fates are kind and grant him the added glory of a Deccan sunset, he will surely return content.

The best base from which to see what remains of the city to day, 350 years since its destruction, is Kāmalāpur [see the Map], seven miles from Hospet railway station (Madras and Southern Mahratta Railway), where a deserted temple was converted into a dwelling by Mr. J H. Master, a former Collector of the district, is now used as a Travellers' Resthouse*

* The Resthouse is fully furnished and the servant in charge of it is capable of preparing meals for visitors, but the only food supplies that can be obtained locally are milk, eggs, fowls, mutton and rice. All other food supplies required should be obtained before leaving Hospet where there is one of Spencer's Refreshment Rooms at the railway station.

Fig. 3.—Natural Archway on the road to Hampi.

and is available to the general public. The only means of conveyance available locally for the journey, are country pony-carts (jutkas) and bullock-carts which can be engaged at Hospet railway station.

Hospet Town.

The town of Hospet was built by Krishna Dēva Rāya, the greatest of all the Vijayanagar kings, between 1509 and 1520 in honour of Nāgalā Dēvi, a courtesan whom he had known in the days of his youth and whom he married after he became king. He called it, after her, Nāgalāpur, and it was his favourite residence. In his time it was the entrance gate, as it were, to the city of Vijayanagar for all travellers coming up from Goa and the west coast. Krishna Dēva also made the enormous embankment south of the town which connects the two ends of the two parallel ranges of hills which further south enclose the valley of Sandur. It was carried out with the aid of a Portuguese Engineer. whose services had been lent to the king by the Governor of Goa. Along the top of it now runs the main road to the taluks of Hadagalli, Harpanahalli and Kūdligi. This great work will be referred to again, under the heading of Irrigation Works.

The modern town of Hospet contains nothing of any antiquarian interest and there is hardly a trace of the old fortified walls that once enclosed the original town of Nāgalāpur.

To the south-east of Hospet is the bold peak of Jambunāth Konda (2,980 feet above the sea) and half way up this, in a picturesque glen, standing on a broad artificial terrace is the temple of Jambunāth. From Hospet to the foot of the hill is about three miles, and a paved way leads up to the temple. Halfway up the ascent is a mandapa on two of the pillars of which are inscriptions. One of these is dated A.D. 1549, and records gifts to the Hanumanta and Anantasayana shrines on the hill. The temple itself is of no particular interest but contains a mineral spring which is accredited with manifold healing virtues.

Soon after the visitor leaves Hospet on his way to Kāmalāpur, he passes through the untidy village of Anantasayanagudi. On the south side of the village is the large and curiously shaped temple of Anantasayana, described in *Part II.* Ruined shrines and mandapas, now begin to appear alongside of the roadway, marking the old route between the inner citadel at Hampi and the suburb of Nāgalāpur, while conspicuous objects to the north are the old square Muhammadan tombs at Kadirānpuram. The Portuguese traveller Paes who visited Vijayanagar in the sixteenth century says that in his time all this road was "a street as wide as a place of tourney, with both sides lined throughout with rows of houses and shops where they sell everything; and all along this road are many trees that the king commanded to be planted, so as to afford shade to those that pass along." Both houses and trees have long since disappeared.

On the left-hand side of the road, close to the fourth mile stone as one proceeds to Kāmalāpur, is a large stone-built well with a flight of steps leading down to the water. It is called the "Soolai Bhavi" and is said to have been built by a dancing-girl for the benefit of travellers passing along this road.

Kāmalāpur. On nearing Kāmalāpur, the road runs along the top of the embankment of the large and beautiful Kāmalāpur tank which is full of fish and provides very fair duck and snipe shooting during the cold weather months. The tank is fed by the Rāya channel from the Tungabhadra and irrigates some 450 acres of wet land, cultivated mainly with rice and sugarcane.

With the exception of the large temple of Pattābhi Rāma which is situated half a mile to the east of the village on the road to Bellary, and a small ruined Poligar fort with a high round tower in the centre, circular bastions at the four corners, and other bastions in the middle of the walls connecting these, Kāmalāpur does not contain any buildings of archæological interest. The more notable of the ruins of the fortifications, temples and buildings of Vijayanagar lie along two roads leading out of this village. The first of these runs north-eastwards to Kampli and the other goes north-west to Hampi and then degenerates into a footpath along the bank of the Tungabhadra.

The greater part of the more interesting buildings are situated in the citadel or innermost line of fortifications and also alongside of the road to Hampi. An account of these will be found in *Part II*.

THE HISTORY OF VIJAYANAGAR FROM THE INSCRIPTIONS.

If legendary history and local tradition be credited, there was a town on this site many centuries before the Vijayanagar kings selected it for their capital. Some of the most dramatic scenes in the great epic of the Rāmāyana occurred at a place called Kishkindha, and it is asserted by the local Brāhmans and generally acknowledged * by the learned in such matters that this Kishkindha was close to Hampi. It was ruled in those early days, says the Rāmāyana, by two brothers of the monkey race called Vāli and Sugriva. They quarrelled and Sugriva was driven out by his brother and fled with Hanumān, the famous monkey-chief of the poem, who had been one of his ministers, to the woods of the hill Rishyamūka, on the bank of the Pampā near the dwelling place of the holy rishi Matanga on the mountain called Matanga Parvatam [see Fig. 4]. Here he was safe from Vāli, for the rishi, furious at finding close to his hermitage the putrefying body of a rākshasa, or demon whom Vāli had killed and flung there, had pronounced a dreadful curse upon him if ever he should again enter that region.

Rāma, the hero of the poem, accompanied by his brother Lakshmana, is journeying south in search of his lovely wife Sita, who has been carried off by Rāvana, the ten-headed demon king of Lanka, or Ceylon, when he is informed that Sugriva can give him news of her. He goes to Rishyamūka and meets Sugriva and Hanumān. The former tells him how he saw Sita being carried through the air by Rāvana and how she dropped one of her garments and her jewels; and how he had retained these latter in a cave. He brings them and shows them to Rāma in proof of the truth of his story. Rāma in his gratitude for this clue slays Vāli with his arrow, burns his huge body on a funeral pyre and replaces Sugriva on the throne. While Rāma waits on Prasravana, a part of the Mālyavanta hill close by, Hanumān searches for Sita, finds her in Lanka, brings back tokens from her to reassure Rāma and finally organizes the monkey army which builds the causeway

* See Rice's *Mysore* I, 277, and the authorities there quoted. Also Dr. Bhandarkar in Bombay Gazetteer, Vol. I, pt. 2, p. 142.

Fig. 4.—Matanga Parvatam and the Soolai Bazaar.

from Rāmēsvaram to Ceylon by which Rāma crosses to the island to the rescue of his bride.

Such is the story in the Rāmāyana, and the names of several of the localities round Hampi are identical with those in the poem. Pampāsaras or Pampāturtham is the name of a tank on the Nizam's side of the Tungabhadra near Ānegundi and Pampā is also said to be the ancient and purānic name of the river; Rishyamūka is the hill on the Nizam's side of the narrowest of the gorges in the river already mentioned; Matanga Parvatam, or Matanga's hill, has been referred to above; Mālyavanta hill (see the Map) lies to the east of it; the cave where Sugriva kept Sita's jewels and the mark made on the rocks by her garment as it fell to earth are pointed out to the pious pilgrim near the river bank; while a curious mound of cinders near the neighbouring hamlet of Nimbāpuram is shown as the cremated remains of Vāli. Enthusiasts go even further and declare that the black-faced grey langurs and the little red-faced monkeys which still scamper and chatter about the hills are the descendants, respectively, of Vāli and Sugriva, and the tumbled masses of fallen boulders which encumber the site of Vijayanagar are the remains of the material collected by Hanumān's monkey hosts for the great causeway. Hanumān is at any rate the most popular deity in the whole district.

The Muhammadan advance, A.D. 1310.

But it is time to return to more sober chronicles. About A.D. 1310, a year which is one of the great landmarks in South Indian chronicles, the advance of the Muhammadans from the north began to seriously threaten the very existence of all Hindu dominion in the south. Malik Kāfur, the famous general of Allā-ud-dīn of the Khilji dynasty of Delhi, swept into the Deccan with an immense force, captured Orangal (Warangal) in the Nizam's Dominions and took and sacked Dvārasamudra. Two years later his armies again marched south and Dēvagiri fell. Both the Hoysalas and the Yādavas were practically extinguished.

Foundation of Vijayanagar, A.D 1336.

Anarchy followed, Mussalman governors, representatives of the old royal families and local chiefs struggling for supremacy, until out of the confusion arose the great Hindu empire of Vijayanagar, which from its capital near Hampi for two centuries remained a bulwark against Muhammadan invasion.

Most authorities agree that the Vijayanagar empire was founded about A.D. 1336, immediately on the disappearance of the Hoysalas from the stage of history, the founders being two Hindu princes named Hakka and Bukka, sons of Sangama. The former became the first king, taking the name of Harihara, and his brother succeeded him. They were probably subordinates of or connected with the Hoysalas, and were aided in their enterprise by the head of the *matha* at Sringēri (in the Kadūr district of Mysore), founded by the reformer Sankarāchārya in the eighth century. The name of this *guru* was Mādhava and he is known as Vidyāranya. He became the first minister of the new State.

The first or Sangama dynasty of Vijayanagar, who were Yādavas, held the throne from 1336 to 1478, and consisted of nine kings. The throne was then usurped by a Sāluva chief, who was succeeded by his son. There were thus only two kings of the Sāluva dynasty, also Yādavas, and they occupied the throne from 1478 to 1496. Then followed the Narasinga dynasty from Tuluva, which ruled from 1496 to 1567, and had six kings. The fourth and last dynasty was the Rāma-Rāja or Karnāta. It was in power from 1567 to 1644, and numbered six kings. It was from a member of this line that the English received in A.D. 1639 a grant of the site of Madras.

Sangama Dynasty, A.D. 1336-1478.

Of Sangama's five sons, the eldest, called according to tradition Hakka, assumed the name of Harihara, and was the first king of the new empire. Kampa or Kampanna became ruler of a kingdom in the east, in the direction of Nellore, and had Sāyana, the commentator on the Vēdas, brother of Mādhava, as his minister. Bukka succeeded Harihara on the throne, and was the most distinguished of the brothers.

The Vijayanagar kings had Virūpāksha for their family god, and their crest was the Varāha or Boar [see Fig. 5], which had been that of the Chālukyas before them. Their capital was probably at first situated at Anegundi on the northern bank of the Tungabhadra nearly opposite the present hamlet of Hampi. As the empire grew in size and power, the capital was moved to the southern bank of the river and Ānegundi was retained as a fortified suburb or outpost.

Of Harihara I, not much is known beyond what has been cited above. But Bukka Rāya, whom he appointed as his

Yuvarāja, was famous. With the assistance of Vidyātīrthamuni he became very great, and "having freed from enemies a hundred royal cities, counting from Dōrasamudra, ruled over an empire perfect in its seven parts." Though the establishment of the capital is attributed to Harihara, and his

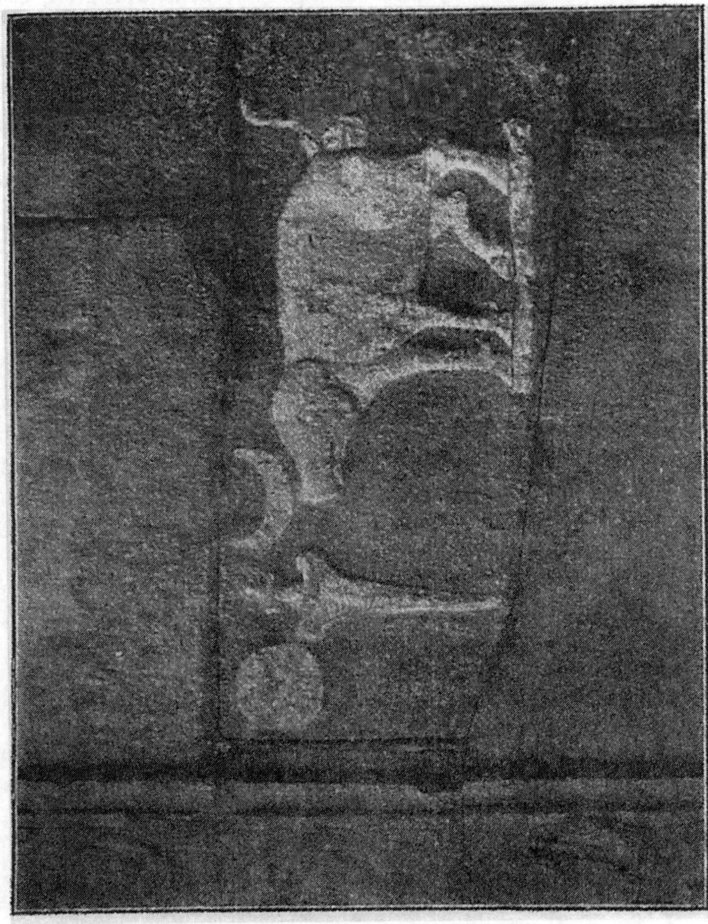

FIG. 5.—VARĀHA OR BOAR CREST OF THE VIJAYANAGAR KINGS.

naming it Vidyānagari after Vidyāranyasrīpāda, the building of the city and the transformation of its name to Vijayanagari or city of victory, are said to have been the work of Bukka Rāya. In the old inscriptions, the latter has the special titles "Destroyer of hostile kings," "Champion over kings who break their word," "Sultan over the Hindu Kings," "Master of the eastern, western and southern oceans." He was a terror to the Turushkas, the Konkana (king) Śankapārya, the Āndhras, Gurjaras, and Kāmbhōjas, and defeated the Kalingas. An interesting event of his reign, showing his liberal-mindedness, was his reconciliation of the Jains and the Vaishnavas in 1368. The latter had been persecuting the former, who in a general body appealed to the king for protection. He summoned the leaders of both sects before him, and declared that no difference could be made between them. Then taking the hand of a Jain and placing it in the hand of a Vaishnava he ordained that they should each pursue their own religious practices with equal freedom. Copies of this decree were set up in various places and still exist.

Harihara II, Bukka Rāya's son by Gaurāmbikā, succeeded him on the throne. But he also had other sons—Virūpanna Odeyar, whose succession was apparently desired in the west; Mallinātha or Mallappa Odeyar, who was ruling in the east of Mysore; and Kampanna Odeyar who was ruling in the south of Mysore. Harihara II is principally praised for making the sixteen great gifts at various sacred places, localities which show that his dominions extended from the Krishna at Kurnool to Kumbhakōnam in the Tanjore district or even farther south. But severe struggles were going on with the Sultāns of the Bahmani kingdom of Gulbarga, which was founded in 1347, or only eleven years after Vijayanagar. Thus, in 1380, when the Turushkas (Muhammadans) were swarming over the Ādavani (Adoni) hill-fort and kingdom, Mallappa Odeyar's son defeated them, took possession of the fort and kingdom, and handed them to Harihara. In 1384 the Turushkas are said to have come and attacked Kottakonda when the army had gone to the Orangal country. In 1397 we are informed of the exploits of the general Gunda, "into the flames of whose valour the Yavanas, Turushkas, and Āndhras fell like moths." He conquered the Kēralas, Taulavas, Āndhras, and Kutakas, seized their wealth, and gave the spoils to the king. He set up pillars of victory in all the fifty-six countries, and restored the tower at the gateway of the Bēlur temple in Mysore, which

Ganga Sālār, the Turushka from Gulbarga, had come and burnt. Harihara was a cultivator of Karnātaka learning. He died on the 30th of August 1404.

He had a son by Pampā Dēvī, who appears to have reigned next, under the name of Immadi Bukka Rāya or Bukka Rāya II. But the reign was a very short one, of little more than a year. Dēva Rāya or Pratāpa Dēva Rāya, Harihara's son by Mēla Dēvī, of the family of Rāma Dēva, then succeeded. He also had the sons Chikka Rāya Odeyar, ruling in Āraga in the hill country to the west; and Virūpanna or Virūpāksha, who conquered the eastern countries down to Ceylon, and in 1404 appears to have been ruling in Vijayanagar. Perhaps he was a candidate for the throne on the death of his father. But Pratāpa Dēva Rāya gained it, and was crowned on the 7th November 1406. Some inscriptions seem to represent him as the founder of the Pratāpa dynasty.

The struggles with the Muhammadans to the north continued unabated, and the pages of Ferishta are filled with details relating to them. According to him, Dēva Rāya, whom he calls Dewul Roy, was forced to give his daughter in marriage to the Bahmani Sultān Fīrōz Shāh. At the end of his reign Dēva Rāya inflicted a severe defeat upon the Sultān. A great slaughter of the Muhammadans followed, and the Bijāpur country was laid waste with all the treasured resentment of many years. These reverses killed Fīrōz Shāh. But his successor, Ahmed Shāh, drove back the Hindus, and desolated the possessions of Vijayanagar, massacring women and children without mercy. Whenever the number came to 20,000, he halted for three days and made a feast. The Hindus, in desperation, formed a plot against him, from which he escaped by a hair's breadth. Terms were then agreed to, and he retired to his own country, the capital of which he shortly removed from Gulbarga to Bīdar, a hundred miles to the north. Of these affairs there is little indication in the inscriptions, which generally represent the king as ruling a peaceful kingdom.

Dēva Rāya was succeeded by Vijaya Rāya, his son by Dēmāmbikā, but the history is not very clear at this period, and Vijaya Rāya's reign was a short one. He was followed by his son Dēva Rāya II, also called Praudha Dēva Rāya, who had the special title Gajabēntekāra or elephant hunter. His mother was Nārāyanāmbikā, and one inscription describes him as having received the throne from his elder sister, which may perhaps refer to the princess married into the Bahmani family. The kings of Anga, Kannōja, Kāmbōja, Vanga, and Nēpāla are said to have acted as his servants, carrying his umbrella, his chāmara, his stick, or his goblet. He also had 10,000 Mussalman horsemen in his service. He died on the 24th of May 1446. He had a brother Pārvvati Rāya Odeyar, who in 1425 ruled the Terakanāmbi kingdom, in the south of Mysore district.

Dēva Rāya's son Mallikārjuna, also called Immadi Dēva Rāya, next came to the throne, and he was followed by Virūpāksha, the son of Dēva Rāya by Simhalā Dēvi. These were reigns wanting in vigour.

Sāluva Dynasty, A.D. 1478–1496.

We now come to Sāluva Nrisimha, also called Narasinga Rāya Odeyar, the most powerful noble in Karnāta and Telingāna. He was general of the armies of Vijayanagar, and successfully defended it against the Muhammadans. But the influence he thus gained enabled him in 1478, in the reign of Virūpāksha, to usurp the throne. When he was thus king, the Bahmani Sultān again invaded the Vijayanagar territories, and was overrunning the whole country, having advanced so far as to lay siege to the strong fort of Mālūr (Kolar district). Nrisimha took to flight, but afterwards came to terms with the Sultān, who nevertheless marched on to Kānchī (Conjeeveram), and plundered the town and temples. Nrisimha was succeeded by his son Immadi Nrisimha or Immadi Narasinga Odeyar, for whom the earliest date seems to be 1493.

Narasinga Dynasty, A.D. 1496–1567.

This king, however, was murdered in 1496 by the general Narasa or Narasinga. He was of Tuluva descent, and became the founder of the Narasinga dynasty of Vijayanagar.

Narasa is said in several inscriptions to have conquered Chēra, Chōla, and Pāndya, as well as the proud lord of Madhura, the fierce Turushka, the Gajapati king and others, from the banks of the Ganges to Lankā (Ceylon) and from the eastern to the western mountains, he imposed his commands upon all kings. In Rāmēsvaram and other sacred places he from time to time bestowed the sixteen great gifts. He died in 1503.

He was succeeded in turn by three sons, born to him by different mothers. The first of these, Vīra Narasimha or Nrisimha, also called in a few cases Bhujabala Rāya, drew to himself, it is said, the hearts of all from Sētu to Sumēru, and from the eastern to the western mountains, and made all manner of gifts in all the sacred places. His half-brother Krishna Rāya next came to the throne, and was the most powerful and distinguished of the Vijayanagar monarchs. About 1520 he inflicted a severe defeat upon the Muhammadans, in consequence of which a good understanding prevailed between the courts of Vijayanagar and Bijāpur for a considerable time. One of the earliest expeditions of the reign was against Ganga Rāja, the chief of Ummattur (in Mysore district), who had rebelled and claimed Penugonda (Penukonda in the Anantapur district), perhaps as being a Ganga. His main stronghold was on the island of Sivasamudram, at the Falls of the Kāvēri, and parts of the Bangalore district were known as the Sivasamudram country. Krishna Rāya captured his fort at the Falls of the Kāvēri and also took Seringapatam. He extended the limits of the empire until they reached to Cuttack on the east and to Salsette on the west. Krishna Rāya was a great patron of Sanskrit and Telugu literature, and had at his court eight celebrated poets. On his death, Achyuta Rāya, his half-brother, succeeded to the throne. He was profuse in his gifts to the Brāhmans, the records of which are commonly surmounted by a figure of the Vāmana or dwarf incarnation of Vishnu. He established in 1539 a kind of bank for the benefit of Brāhmans, called the Ananda Nidhi. Two verses celebrating this event are recorded in several places at Hampi and Kāmalāpur.

Achyuta Rāya's son, perhaps an infant, was crowned as king, but died in a short time. Sadāsiva Rāya, the son of Ranga, a deceased brother of Achyuta by the same mother, was then raised to the throne by the great minister Rāma Rāja (who was his brother-in-law) and the councillors. He is said to have subdued all his enemies in Suragiri (Penukonda), and brought the whole land into subjection to his commands, while the Kāmbōja, Bhōja, Kalinga, Karahāta and other kings acted as servants for his female apartments. But Rāma

Rāja himself wielded the chief power in the State, and is called the ruler of the great Karnāta kingdom. Though possessed of commanding abilities, so great was his arrogance that the Mussalman States of Bijāpur, Golkonda, Ahmadnagar, and Bīdar were provoked to combine in an attack on Vijayanagar as their common enemy. In the battle of Talikōta, near Raichur, on the 23rd of January 1565, Rāma Rāja was slain, on which the Hindu army fled panic-stricken, and the royal family escaped to the fort at Penukonda. The victorious Muhammadans marched on to Vijayanagar, which they utterly sacked and destroyed. Thus fell this once great and populous capital, the ruins of which are still a source of wonder and admiration to visitors.

Karnāta Dynasty. A.D. 1567–1644.

From Rāma Rāja was descended the last Vijayanagar dynasty, styling themselves kings of Karnāta. Their capital was first at Penukonda, which was attacked in 1577 by the Muhammadans, but successfully defended by Jagadēva Rāya, whose daughter was married to the king, and who became chief of Channapatna. In 1585 the capital was removed to Chandragiri [see Fig. 6], and later still to Chingleput. These were, however, captured by the forces of Golkonda, and the king fled to the protection of Sivappa Nāyak, the chief of Bednūr in the west of Mysore. The line eventually merged into that of the chiefs of Ānegundi, who were subdued by Tipū Sultān.

Muhammadan influence.

The Muhammadan invasion and especially the employment of Muhammadan troops by the Vijayanagar kings led to Saracenic features being adopted in some of the buildings in their capital, producing an Indian version of that style, known as Indo-Saracenic. Examples of buildings in this style are dealt with in *Part II*. The chronicle of Fernão Nuniz, a Portuguese traveller who visited Vijayanagar during the reign of Krishna Dēva Rāya, records that the king requested the Governor of Goa to depute some Portuguese stone masons to come to Vijayanagar to superintend the building of a large water reservoir that he desired to construct near Hospet, and that the Governor sent him Joao della Ponte "a great worker in stone." Nuniz relates that when this engineer requested the king to have a large quantity of lime prepared for the work, "the king laughed much, for in his country when they

Portuguese influence.

build a house they do not understand how to use lime." If this statement of Nuniz is correct, the Hindus of Southern India are indebted to the Portuguese for the introduction of the use of a very valuable building material. It is certainly a

FIG. 6.—THE PALACE AT CHANDRAGIRI.

fact that very few traces of lime mortar are discernible between the joints of the stonework of the earlier buildings at Vijayanagar, except in these buildings which have been repaired at a later date. But the Hindus certainly understood the use of mortar in the treatment of brickwork long before they came in contact with the Portuguese. However, they do not seem to have made much use of their knowledge of this valuable material when erecting buildings in stone prior to the sixteenth century. It may be that, as a rule, the blocks of stone used in constructing the temples, basements of palaces, and many other buildings at Vijayanagar, were so large and heavy, and so beautifully dressed and accurately fitted together, that no cementing material was considered necessary.

SOCIAL AND POLITICAL HISTORY AS RECORDED BY FOREIGN VISITORS TO VIJAYANAGAR.

Foreign visitors to Vijayanagar.

Although it is impossible to underrate the historical value of the old inscriptions relating to the Vijayanagar dynasties, records of this kind do not, as a rule, give one much information concerning the social and political affairs of the country at the different periods to which the inscriptions relate. So if we desire a picture of Vijayanagar in its palmy days we must turn to the old chronicles of the European travellers who visited the city before its destruction by the Muhammadans in A.D. 1565.

During the reign of Dēva Rāya II two foreigners visited his capital. The first of these was Nicolo Conti, an Italian, who came there about 1420, and the second was Abdur Razzāk, an ambassador from Persia, who followed some twenty years later. Both of them have left glowing accounts of the richness and magnificence of the city and certain extracts from these will be found in the account of the buildings which is given in *Part II.* Conti states that insolvent debtors became the property of their creditors, mentions the practice of sati or widow burning, and hook-swinging as being in vogue, and says that at the car festivals people used to throw themselves under the wheels of the car, "a mode of death which they say is very acceptable to their god." The feasts of the Canarese New Year's Day, the Dipāvali, Holi and the Dasara festivals were also kept. Abdur Razzāk gives a very vivid account of the celebration of one of these and also describes the buildings about the king's palace which has proved of great assistance in identifying the various portions of it which are still traceable. He says the kingdom extended from the Kistna (Krishna) river to Cape Comorin.

Krishna Dēva Rāya, A.D. 1509–1530. His personality.

Krishna Dēva Rāya stands out more conspicuously on the stage of history than any other ruler of Vijayanagar, and under him the empire reached the zenith of its power. The chronicle of Domingos Paes, a Portuguese, who visited Vijayanagar about 1520, which has been made available by Mr. Sewell * gives us many graphic details of his personality. He was an athlete and kept himself in hard "condition" by regular bodily exercise, rising early and practising sword-play or riding about the plains round the city before sunrise. He had a noble presence, attractive manners and a strong personal influence over those about him. He led his armies in person and yet was a poet and a patron of literature. Able, brave and statesmanlike he was withal a man of much gentleness and generosity of character.

His buildings.

He did more than any of his predecessors to beautify his capital, building in it the ranga-mandapa and eastern gateway of the Pampāpati temple, the Krishna and Hazāra Rāma temples and the great monolithic statue of Narasimha, and beginning the famous temple to Vitthala. As an inscription near it testifies, he made the anicut on the Tungabhadra at Vallabhāpuram and the Basavanna irrigation channel which takes off from it and perhaps constructed others of the Tungabhadra channels. He erected the huge embankment near Hospet at the north-western end of the two ranges of hills which enclose the State of Sandur and he built the town of Hospet in honour of a courtesan named Nāgalā Dēvi as already related above.

His administrative improvements.

He systematized the organization of the empire, which was divided into a number of provinces each under a local governor, who was responsible for its administration, paid from its revenues a certain fixed annual contribution to the royal exchequer, kept up a fixed number of troops ready for immediate service on behalf of the king, and retained for his own use such revenues as remained after satisfying these

* "A Forgotten Empire," by Robert Sewell, Swan Sonnenschein & Co., Ltd., London.

conditions. He was thus enabled to raise the enormous armies which he led against his enemies and to erect a number of costly buildings in his capital.

His patronage of literature.

He greatly encouraged literature and gathered about his court the best poets of his time. He was himself a poet, composing in Sanskrit and Telugu. None of his Sanskrit works have survived, but a Telugu poem of his called *Amuktha-mālyada* or *Vishnu Chiththiyamu* is pronounced by competent authority to be an excellent production. Until Krishna Dēva's time, Telugu poetry had been confined to versions in that language of the classical Sanskrit works, such as the Rāmāyana and the Mahābhārata, but thenceforth original poems began to be composed. The originator of this advance was Allasāni Peddana, the chief of the poets at Krishna Dēva's court and to this day one of the most popular and best known of Telugu versifiers.

His military expeditions to Mysore and the East Coast.

Krishna Dēva's victories in war were no less renowned than his triumphs in peace. Soon after his accession he reduced to order a refractory vassal in Mysore, capturing the two strong fortresses of Sivasamudram and Seringapatam, both built on islands in the middle of the Cauvery river. In 1513 he marched against the hill fortress of Udayagiri in the Nellore district, then under the king of Orissa, captured it and brought from it the image of Krishna which was set up in the Krishna temple in his capital.* In 1515 he took Kondavedu in the Guntūr district and Kondapalle in the Kistna district, two very strong hill fortresses, and Rajahmundry in the Gōdāvari district. He thus consolidated his possessions on the east coast of the Presidency.

His capture of Raichūr and the Doāb.

In 1520 he set out against Raichūr, the fortress in the debatable land which for nearly two centuries had been the subject of dispute between his predecessors and their northern neighbours. It belonged at this time to Ismāil Ādil Shah, the king of Bijāpur. According to Fernão Nuniz, the second of the two Portuguese chroniclers whose narratives Mr. Sewell has brought to light, the army he took with him numbered as many as 736,000 men with 550 elephants, and advanced in eleven great divisions. He began a regular siege of Raichūr

* This image is now in the Madras Museum.

and Ismail marched out with 140,000 horse and foot to relieve the place. A tremendous battle took place between Raichūr and the Kistna river. Krishna Dēva opened the engagement by a frontal attack in massed formation and drove in the Bijāpur centre, but the enemy directed a devastating fire upon the Hindus from guns which had been held in reserve in the rear and following up their advantage with a cavalry charge routed them and pursued them for a mile and a half. Krishna Dēva, however, in person rallied and led forward his second line and fell upon the Mussalmans with such impetuosity that he drove them right back into the river, where immense slaughter took place. He then crossed the river and attacked the camp of Ismāil Ādil Shah, who barely escaped with his life. The result of the action was decisive and Ismāil never again attacked the Vijayanagar territories while Krishna Dēva was alive. Krishna Dēva returned from the battle and resumed the siege of Raichūr, which he soon captured. His success here was in no small measure due to the marksmanship of some Portuguese mercenaries, who with their arquebuses picked off the defenders on the walls and so enabled the besiegers to approach close to the lines of fortification and breach them. The great battle and siege are most vividly described by Nuniz, who appears to have been himself present at both.

His haughty treatment of the Mussalmans.

Krishna Dēva was unduly uplifted by his successes. He despatched haughty and irritating replies to the other Muhammadan kings of the Deccan who sent envoys to him, and to Ismāil Ādil Shah's ambassador he gave answer that if the king would come and kiss his foot, his lands and fortress would be restored to him. This overbearing behaviour was the first item in the long list of insults and humiliations received at the hands of the rulers of Vijayanagar which eventually induced the Muhammadan kings of the Deccan to forget their own differences in order to unite and crush their common enemy.

Achyuta Rāya, A.D. 1530–1542.

Krishna Dēva Rāya died in 1530 and was succeeded by Achyuta, his half-brother. Achyuta was a craven and withal a tyrant. He alienated his best friends by his violent despotism and his conduct and mode of government ruined the Hindu cause in Southern India and opened the country to the invader, though he himself did not live to see the end. Ismāil

Ādil Shah of Bijāpur speedily took his measure and attacked Mudkal and Raichūr and captured them.

Bijāpur king visits Vijayanagar.

About 1535, however, Ismāil's successor, Ibrahim Ādil Shah, came to Vijayanagar itself and was received in friendly fashion by Achyuta. How this came about is not clear. Ferishta says that the Vijayanagar nobles were driven by Achyuta's tyrannies into open revolt and that the king actually had to send for his hereditary foe from Bijāpur to protect him, promising in return to declare Vijayanagar tributary to Bijāpur. The nobles, more patriotic than their king, prayed Achyuta to dismiss Ibrahim, promising obedience if only he were removed. Achyuta eventually gave Ibrahim some two millions sterling and he returned to his own country. The whole episode is most extraordinary.

The three brothers.

Immediately after Ibrahim had retired, the rebellious nobles reasserted their influence and Achyuta was thenceforth king in little but name. The chief of the recalcitrants were three brothers named Rāma Rāja, Tirumala and Venkatādri. The two first had married daughters of Krishna Dēva. Rāma Rāja was the most prominent of the three and Ferishta indeed speaks of him henceforth as if he were in fact king of Vijayanagar.

Sadāsiva nominally King, A.D. 1542–1567.

Achyuta died in 1542 and was nominally succeeded by Sadāsiva, who was perhaps his nephew. The new ruler was, however, kept under restraint the whole of his life and all real power lay in the hands of the three brothers already mentioned, though they professed allegiance to the nominal king.

Rāma Rāja's dealings with the Mussalmans.

Rāma Rāja did much to repair the blunders of Achyuta and rehabilitate the prestige of Vijayanagar. His favourite method seems to have been to play off one of the Muhammadan kings against another so as to keep them from uniting. In 1557, the Bijāpur king went in person to Vijayanagar with the hope of establishing a lasting friendship with Rāma Rāja, but the latter treated him with such scant respect that the effect of the visit was rather to estrange the two than bring them together. In the next year, however, they combined against the king of Ahmadnagar and between them ravaged the whole of his dominions. "The infidels of Vijayanagar," says Ferishta, "left no cruelty unpractised.

They insulted the honour of the Mussalman women, destroyed the mosques, and did not even respect the sacred Korān." Their behaviour infuriated their friends no less than their enemies and made one more item in the long account which the Muhammadans already had against them. Shortly afterwards Ahmadnagar and Golkonda combined to attack Bijāpur, whose king again applied to Rāma Rāja for help. A battle ensued but the Golkonda king deserted Ahmadnagar, who was then driven by the three allies into his capital. The Hindus again committed all manner of excess, "burning and razing buildings," says Ferishta, "putting up their horses in the mosques and performing their idolatrous worship in the holy places." Rāma Rāja's behaviour to the Mussalmans was more insufferable than ever. "Looking on the Islām Sultāns as of little consequence, he refused proper honours to their ambassadors. When he admitted them to his presence, he did not suffer them to sit, and treated them with the most contemptuous reserve and haughtiness. He made them attend when in public in his train on foot, not allowing them to mount until he gave orders." He moreover despatched large armies to the frontiers of Golkonda and Bijāpur.

The Muhammadans combine against Vijayanagar.

The Muhammadan kings could at length no longer brook his arrogance and sinking their own animosities they formed "a general league of the faithful against him." On Christmas Day, 1564, they began their united advance southward and halted near the town and fortress of Talikōta, 25 miles north of the Kistna river. Rāma Rāja despatched his brother Tirumala with 20,000 horse, 100,000 foot and 500 elephants to block the passage of the river, then sent off his other brother Venkatādri with another large force, and finally marched in person to the point of attack with the whole remaining power of the Vijayanagar empire. His total force is said to have numbered 600,000 foot and 100,000 horse. The Hindus had fortified their side of the ford opposite the enemy's camp, but the latter drew them off by pretending to attempt another passage, and then returning suddenly to the original ford crossed it unopposed. They then marched south towards Rāma Rāja's camp.

The battle Talikōta, A.D. 1565.

On the 23rd January 1565 the great battle of Talikōta (as it was called), one of the most decisive battles in all South

Indian history, was fought. All the available forces on either side took part in it. Rāma Rāja, though over ninety years of age, commanded the Vijayanagar centre and his brother Tirumala and Venkatādri led, respectively, the left and right divisions. The Muhammadans awaited the attack with their artillery in the centre, opposite Rāma Rāja's division. This consisted of six hundred pieces of ordnance disposed in three lines, the heavy artillery in front, then the smaller pieces, and in the rear light swivel guns. Masking all these were two thousand archers. These latter kept up a heavy fire as the enemy advanced and then falling rapidly back allowed the massed batteries to open fire. Their effect was murderous and decisive, and the Hindus retreated in disorder. On the flanks they had, however, been more successful and had driven back the Mussalmans, and the centre rallied for a charge upon the guns. At first their onslaught seemed to prevail, but the Mussalmans' heavy guns, loaded with bags of copper coin, were fired into them at close quarters, 5,000 of them fell, and the Mussalman cavalry charged through the intervals of the guns and cut their way straight through the disorganized masses of the enemy right up to where Rāma Rāja was posted.

Rāma Rāja had at first superintended operations from a litter. Later, thinking to encourage his men, he seated himself on a "rich throne set with jewels, under a canopy of crimson velvet embroidered with gold and adorned with fringes of pearls," from whence he distributed money, gold and jewels to those of his followers who acquitted themselves well. Later again, he returned to his litter and it was at this moment that the Mussalman cavalry charged up to his position. One of the enemy's elephants stampeded towards him, his bearers dropped him and fled, and before he could mount a horse he was taken prisoner. He was taken before the king of Ahmadnagar, who immediately had his head cut off and raised on a long spear so that the Hindu troops might see it.

This disaster caused an instant panic among the Vijayanagar forces and they broke and fled. "They were pursued," says Ferishta, "by the allies with such successful slaughter that the river which ran near the field was dyed red with their blood. It is computed on the best authorities that above 100,000 infidels were slain in fight and during the pursuit."

Their panic was so great that they made no attempt to rally on a fresh position or even to defend the hills and approaches round about their capital. Venkatādri had been slain and of the three brothers Tirumala alone remained. He hastily returned to Vijayanagar and fled thence with the puppet king Sadāsiva to the hill fort of Penukonda in the Anantapur district, taking with him a few followers and a convoy of 550 elephants laden with treasure in gold, diamonds and precious stones valued at more than 100 millions sterling and also the state insignia and the celebrated jewelled throne.

Deserted by their king and the commandant of their troops, the people of the capital made no effort to defend themselves and the very next day the city was looted by hordes of wandering gipsies—Lambādis and the like. On the third day the victorious Muhammadans arrived and for five months "with fire and sword, with crowbars and axes," to quote Mr. Sewell, * "they carried on day after day their work of destruction. Never perhaps in the history of the world has such havoc been wrought, and wrought so suddenly, on so splendid a city; teeming with a wealthy and industrious population in the full plenitude of prosperity one day, and on the next seized, pillaged, and reduced to ruins, amid scenes of savage massacre and horrors beggaring description."

Two years later, Caesaro Federici, an Italian traveller, visited the place and wrote of it that "the houses stand still but emptie, and there is dwelling in them nothing, as is reported, but Tygres and other wild beasts." Thus Vijayanagar as a city was blotted out, and has never since been inhabited by any but the few cultivators who still till the fields which wind about among its deserted streets and temples.

On the fall of the capital, anarchy followed throughout the dominions of the empire. Sadāsiva and Tirumala kept up a certain state at Penukonda, but the nobles for the most part threw off their allegiance to them and proclaimed themselves independent.

---

* "A Forgotten Empire," p. 208.

In 1568 Tirumala murdered Sadāsiva and seized the throne for himself. A few years later he was forced to fly to Chandragiri in the Chittoor district, and it was there that one of his descendants in 1639 granted to Francis Day the land on which Fort Saint George in Madras now stands. The existing representative of the family is the Rāja of Ānegundi, a place in the Nizam's Dominions nearly opposite to Hampi.

Of all the accounts of Vijayanagar in the height of its power, that of Domingos Paes, which Mr. Sewell has given us in his history of this "Forgotten Empire," is the most vivid and picturesque. Space will not admit of the reproduction of his description here and to curtail it is to ruin it. The reader who desires a picture of the Vijayanagar of those days should peruse Paes' story as it stands in Mr. Sewell's work.

RELIGION.

Jainism. From the architectural style of a few of the smaller stone temples situated on Hēmakutam, the hill immediately to the south of the great Pampāpati temple at Hampi [see the Map], it would appear that the Jains were in occupation of this site long before the founding of Vijayanagar by the Hindus in the fourteenth century. We also learn from the inscriptions, as already mentioned above, that in the reign of Bukka Rāya, as early as 1368, the king brought about a reconciliation between the Jains and the Vaishnavas, as the latter had been persecuting the former. The fact that Bukka Rāya ordained that "they should each pursue their own religious practices with equal freedom," tends to show that the Jains at that period were an important and influential community. The ruins of their temples at Hampi, and also those scattered throughout the Bellary district show how widely the Jaina faith must formerly have prevailed. Even to-day, a few Jains occur in the district but their numbers are very small and their influence upon the religious life of the district is now a negligible quantity. A description of the Jain temples at Hampi will be found in *Part II.*

Hinduism. The oldest and most sacred Hindu temple at Hampi is the Pampāpati temple already mentioned above. In erecting Hindu temples in early times, it was not an uncommon practice of the Brāhmans, when possible, to select a site on, or adjacent to, some former sacred spot of the Buddhists or the Jains which had already acquired a considerable reputation for sanctity. It is possible that the Jains had a temple on this site long before the founding of the kingdom of Vijayanagar in 1336, and that they were driven from it by the Hindus which led to the reconciliation of the two sects in 1368, mentioned above.

The Pampāpati temple, as it stands to-day, is a collection of buildings erected at different periods. The little shrine to Bhuvanēsvari, for instance, is built in the Chālukyan style of about the eleventh or twelfth century—that is, it belongs to a period anterior to the founding of Vijayanagar. We know from the inscriptions that although the Vijayanagar kings built innumerable temples in honour of the great Hindu deities Śiva and Vishnu, they retained Virūpāksha (a form of Śiva) as their family, or tutelary, god, and it seems certain that the first temple which they built, or otherwise acquired at Hampi in 1336, was dedicated to this particular deity. Even now the Pampāpati temple is also known by the name of Virūpāksha. The word Pampā is usually said to have been the ancient and purānic name of the river Tungabhadra, on the southern bank of which the temple in question stands. The local historians, however, favour another version which says that Pampā was a daughter of Brahma who was wont to bring fruit and flowers to the holy rishis who in olden times lived on Hēmakutam. Pleased with her faithful service they asked her to name a boon in return. She replied that she wished to wed Virūpāksha. Taught by the rishis, she did such penance that Virūpāksha looked with favour upon her, espoused her, and took the name of Pampāpati or lord of Pampā, under which, and also under the name of Virūpāksha, he is still worshipped in this temple.

Whichever version is preferred, the fact remains that the word Pampā has given the village and the ruins the name by which they are now known. For Hampe (as it should properly be spelt) is a corruption of Pampā, the initial P of the old Canarese changing, as it often does into H.

Tree and Serpent Worship.

A very popular form of religion and one which prevailed particularly during the Vijayanagar period, was the worship of trees and snakes, and it is possible that Virūpāksha was mainly worshipped in this connection. In his original form, Virūpāksha was regarded as the Lord of the Nāgas (Serpents), the red king who ruled over the western quarter. In the old Buddhist legends, the Nāgas are fabled to reside under the Trikuta rocks supporting Mount Meru, and also in the waters of springs, lakes and rivers, watching over great treasures, causing rain, certain maladies, and having the power of bestowing offspring on women desiring children. It is in this last connection that the worship of the Nāga seems to have been most popular in early times and also at the present day.

It is the Nāga, or hooded cobra alone that is sacred, and he is generally worshipped on the Nāgula chaviti, or the fourth day of the bright fortnight in the month of Srāvana (July–August), when women fast and pour milk over the nāgakals (snake-stones) or over ant-hills in which cobras are believed to reside. This day is reserved as a great festival and the usual form of serpent worship at the present day, is the vow taken by childless wives to instal a nāgakal (snake-stone) *nāgapratishtai* if they are blessed with offspring. The ceremony consists in having the figure of a cobra carved upon a small stone slab, placing it in water for six months, "giving it life" *prānapratishtai*, by reciting mantrams and other ceremonies over it, and then setting it up under a sacred pipal or margosa tree, or for preference, under the shade of a pipal tree that has been "married" to a margosa tree. These two trees are often planted together "married" as the saying goes—on a raised platform and worshipped by Brāhmans and other high castes.

To what extent, if any, the Vijayanagar kings regarded Virūpāksha in his original form as Lord of the Nāgas, we do not know but some of the existing monuments at Vijayanagar supply abundant evidence that their womenfolk at least, were mainly Nāga worshippers. These women not only set up nāgakals (snake-stones) in the temples which they attended, but they had a regular type of Nāga goddess which they worshipped. In the north-east corner of the so-called Underground temple, the visitor to Hampi will find a great number of nāgakals set up there by women who fulfilled their vows to the Nāga who was supposed to reside in this particular temple [see Fig. 7]. On the verandah of the Travellers' Resthouse at Kāmalāpur, may be seen a carved stone image of a female Nāga or Nāgī [see Fig. 8]. The style of the latter

FIG. 7.—GROUP OF NĀGAKALS IN THE UNDERGROUND TEMPLE.

is different to the ordinary nāgakals. The floriated aureola above the figure's head, the two female attendants, and the fact that the Nāgī is carved on a pitha or pedestal, clearly indicates that it represents an image specially designed as an object of worship and nct as a mere nāgakal. This image

FIG. 8.—IMAGE OF A NĀGĪ, OR SERPENT GODDESS.

appears to represent a veritable queen mother of Nāgas, and just the type of figure the Hindu sculptor might be expected to create if he were called upon to execute an image representing the consort of Virūpāksha in his original form as Lord of the Nāgas. Another image of the same kind, only much inferior in workmanship, may be seen set up in the village of Kāmalāpur with the fallen walls of the temple that once enshrined it clustering about its base [see Fig. 9]. No doubt, this little shrine was wrecked by the Muhammadans who also appear to have had a hand in mutilating the large Nāgī now on the verandah of the Travellers' Resthouse. The latter image was found near the Kodanda Rāma temple and removed to the Resthouse for safety.

Tree and serpent worship is responsible for many decorative emblems in Indian art, such as five and seven-headed serpents, designs representing interlaced serpents resembling wicker-work, and representations of sacred trees and flowers. Bas-relief sculptures depicting Krishna killing a large serpent by crushing its head with his heel; the same god playing on his flute protected from the sun or rain, by a huge many-headed cobra and several other scenes in which the serpent is introduced, may be observed carved upon the walls and pillars of many of the larger temples at Hampi.

The Cult of Vishnu.

In early times, as the worship of Vishnu spread and absorbed many minor cults, it developed thence the idea of avatars (avatāra, 'descent'), i.e., incarnations of a larger or smaller portion of the divine spirit in human or animal form from age to age in order to maintain the order of righteousness in the world.

The incarnations of Vishnu most popular in modern Hinduism are:—

(1) The *Fish*, which saved from the deluge *Manu*, the parent of mankind.

(2) The *Tortoise*, which stood in the "Ocean of Milk" and supported on its back Mount Mandara, with which the gods and demons churned the ocean and thence drew certain mythological treasures.

(3) The *Boar*, which destroyed a demon and raised the submerged earth from the sea.

FIG. 9.—RUINED NĀGĪ SHRINE AT KĀMALĀPUR.

(4) The *Man-lion*, which saved the pious youth *Prahlāda* by slaying his cruel father the demon *Hiranyakasipu*.

(5) The *Dwarf*, who deposed the demon *Bali* from the dominions of the three worlds.

(6) *Parasu Rāma*, the Brāhman hero, who destroyed the Warrior caste.

(7) *Rāma* or *Rāmachandra*.

(8) *Krishna*.

(9) *Buddha*, in order to lure the impious to destruction by the sophistries of Buddhism.

(10) *Kalki*, an incarnation yet to come, in which Vishnu will appear on a white horse with a drawn sword, to restore the order of righteousness.

Sculptured representations of all of these incarnations may be seen carved upon the gateways and also on the pillars and walls of the temples themselves.

The Legend of Rāma.

This myth was one of the many absorbed by the conquering Vaishnava church, and was early made the theme of a great epic, the Rāmāyana, ascribed to the poet Vālmīki.* The Rāmāyana narrates the birth of Rāma or Rāmachandra (embodying half the divine essence), and of his half-brothers, Bharata, Lakshmana, and Satrughna, all of them sons of King Dasaratha of Ayodhyā (near the modern Faizabad); how in his early youth Rāma bent the ponderous bow of King Janaka Videha (Mithilā), and won as prize Janaka's lovely daughter Sītā as his bride; how Rāma, exiled by his father, dwelt with Sītā and Lakshmana in the forest, whence Sītā was carried off by the demon king Rāvana to Lankā (Ceylon); how Rāma, aided by the hosts of the monkey-king, invaded Lankā, destroyed Rāvana and his armies and brought back Sītā to Ayodhyā, where he was crowned as king; how Rāma, moved by foolish gossip of his people, sent Sītā away to the hermitage of Vālmīki, where she bore his two sons Kusa and Lava; and how at length after reunion they were raised to heaven. The story is truly epic, and has an immense influence over the hearts of India, as indeed it deserves. It is read in some version in every village, and it has been made especially the Bible of the Hindi-speaking world by the noble poem of Tulsī Dās (sixteenth century).

The Rāmāyana is responsible for most of the beautiful bas-relief sculpture adorning the walls and pillars of the big

* The nucleus of the poem was composed about 500 B.C., but it has been later recast and expanded.

Vaishnava temples at Hampi. In the Hazāra Rāmachandra temple, the visitor to Hampi will find all the leading incidents in this great epic illustrated in stone.

The Legends of Krishna.

These are no less important in Vaishnava worship than story of Rāma. The chief literary sources are the Mahābhārata with its appendix the Harivamsa, the Pāncharātra, and the Bhāgayata Purāna.

The Mahābhārata is a gigantic collection which began about 500 B.C., as an epic poem commemorating the wars of the Bhāratas (for whom afterwards the Pāndavas were substituted) and the Kauravas; but this original form has been recast and expanded by additions of almost every conceivable kind of matter. In the older parts of the poem Krishna figures simply as a demi-god and king; but in the later portions he is represented as the full incarnation of Vishnu, especially in the Bhagavad-gītā, the most powerful and popular exposition of this aspect of the cult.

According to the legend, Krishna (so called from his black or blue skin) was born as the son of Vasudēva, and was saved from the murderous hands of Kamsa, king of Mathurā, by his father, who gave him into the charge of the herdsman, Nanda. Krishna spent his childhood and youth as a shepherd in Vraja (in Muttra district) about Vrindāvana; and around this period of his life, and especially around his amours with Rādhā and the Gopīs, or herdswomen, a cycle of brilliantly sensuous myths has gathered, which seem hardly known in the Mahābhārata; the most popular record of them is the Bhāgavata Purāna.

Like the Rāmāyana, the Mahābhārata has greatly influenced the ornamentation of the temples at Hampi. Krishna as a boy playing on his flute; Krishna killing a huge serpent by crushing its head with his heel; the same god stealing the butter; also Krishna stealing the clothes of the Gopīs while they were bathing and a host of other scenes from the legends of this popular deity, will be found in great numbers carved upon the walls and pillars of the larger temples.

The Cult of Siva

While Vishnu is the Preserver, the loving guardian of all his creatures amidst the ceaseless change of cosmic life, Śiva, the Rudra of the Vedas, represents the earliest and universal

FIG. 10. LARGE LINGA IN THE RUINED ŚIVA SHRINE NEAR THE NARASIMHA STATUE.

impression of Nature upon men—the impression of endless and pitiless change. He is the destroyer and rebuilder of various forms of life; he has charge of the whole circle of animated creation, the incessant round of birth and death in which all Nature eternally revolves. His attributes are indicated by symbols emblematic of death and of men's desire; he presides over the ebb and flow of sentient existence. In Siva we have the condensation of the two primordial agencies the striving to live and the forces that kill. He exhibits by images, emblems, and allegorical carvings the whole course and revolution of Nature, the inexorable law of the alternate triumph of life and death. Śiva (gracious one) or Mahādeva (great god) is in essence the same as the Vedic Rudra—the god of the wild mountains. Fierce and terrible, he dwells with his bride Pārvati in the heart of Himalaya, attended by goblin bands, often amidst wild revelry. To symbolize the reproductive changes in Nature, he has for token the linga [see Fig. 10], or male organ of generation; and as lord of the spirits of the dead he haunts graveyards wearing garlands of serpents and a necklace of skulls. In a somewhat milder aspect, he appears as a yogi or ascetic saint buried in millennial reverie, typical of the Hindu ascetics who seek by mortifications and abstraction of thought to attain supernatural powers and final union of the soul with the Absolute Spirit.

But horror and even grotesqueness of representation do not prevent an Indian god from winning intense personal love and devotion from his worshippers. As Vishnu in his hideous form of Narasimha (the Man-lion incarnation), so Siva in all his legendary ugliness—naked, blue of throat and red of skin, or livid white, three-eyed, besmeared with ashes and cow-dung—is often invested by devout and refined imaginations with attributes of supreme sweetness and love.

Sati or Widow Burning.

The group of sati memorials, shown in Fig. 11, are situated on the western side of the main road to Hampi and outside the small temple of Uddāna Vīrabhadra close to Krishnapuram.

The practice of sati, or the burning of a widow with the dead body of her husband, was a recognized institution in India at all periods, but it seems to have been more actively revived in the fourteenth century under the Vijayanagar kings than at any other period. The memorials of sati

FIG. 11.—SATI MEMORIALS ON THE ROAD TO HAMPI.

which was entered on with perfect readiness, as duty-bound in honour, are found in all parts. They are particularly numerous in Mysore and the Madras Presidency. As a rule, a sculptured representation of the widow or widows who committed sati is carved on the stone memorial to the dead husband in the manner shown here in Fig. 11. This type of memorial is generally known as a vīrakal or hero-stone, and in Southern India, they appear to have been set up chiefly in honour of feudal chiefs and nobles of the Vijayanagar empire who were slain in battle or killed in some hunting expedition. Some of these memorials, however, were set up mainly in honour of those who committed sati, and these are known as māstikal, that is maha-sati-kal, or great sati-stone, and are generally sculptured with a pointed pillar or post, from which projects a woman's right arm, bent upwards at the elbow. The hand is raised, with fingers erect, and a lime-fruit is usually shown placed between the thumb and forefinger. This is what is alluded to in the old inscriptions, where women are said to "have given arm and hand." Some of these memorials are accompanied with elaborate inscriptions. Unfortunately, the few vīrakals at Hampi are not inscribed but we may feel quite sure that they were erected in honour of persons of rank and distinction. In the lower panels, we have a crude sculptured representation of the departed hero, with hands raised in prayer, accompanied by the wife or wives who committed sati on his death. The female figures are depicted with the right arm and hand raised in the manner related above. In the upper panel is a representation of a linga on its yoni pedestal and a figure of the bull Nandi, denoting that the departed hero was a worshipper of Śiva. In the upper panel of one vīrakal, the husband and wife are depicted seated together before the peculiar emblems of the Saivite faith. Whilst in another vīrakal the hero is shown making offerings of garlands of flowers to the linga. Above the topmost panel are usually carved representations of the sun and moon, denoting that the testimony of the stone will last for ever. The sati memorial, illustrated in Fig. 12, is situated in front of the so-called Jaina temple on the bank of the river, halfway between Hampi and the Vitthala temple. The lower panel represents

FIG. 12.—SATI MEMORIAL IN FRONT OF THE JAINA TEMPLE BY THE RIVER.

the hero and his two wives who committed sati on his death. To the left is the hero's elephant in charge of an attendant. This appears to have been included by the sculptor merely to show that the hero was a person of rank, in the same manner as they often portray a horse or an umbrella of state. In the top panel, the hero and his two wives are shown as having arrived in Vishnu's abode of bliss and stand before the sacred conch (shell) and chakram (wheel or discus) emblems of Vishnu which are shown as being adored by Hanumān and Garuda (vehicle of Vishnu) respectively.

The following interesting account of sati as performed in Vijayanagar in the sixteenth century is taken from the

"Chronicle of Fernão Nuniz," published in Mr. Sewell's "Forgotten Empire":—"The women have the custom of burning themselves when their husbands die, and hold it an honour to do so. When, therefore, their husbands die they mourn with their relations and those of their husbands, but they hold that the wife who weeps beyond measure has no desire to go in search of her husband; and the mourning finished, their relations speak to them, advising them to burn themselves and not to dishonour their generation. After that, it is said, they place the dead man on a bed with a canopy of branches and covered with flowers and they put the woman on the back of a worthless horse, and she goes after them with many jewels on her, and covered with roses; she carries a mirror in her hand and in the other a branch of flowers, and (she goes accompanied by) many kinds of music, and his relations (go with her) with much pleasure. A man goes also playing on a small drum and he sings songs to her telling her that she is going to join her husband and she answers also in singing that so she will do. As soon as she arrives at the place where they are always burned she waits with the musicians till her husband is burned, whose body they place in a very large pit that has been made ready for it, covered with much firewood. Before they light the fire his mother or nearest relative takes a vessel of water on the head and a firebrand in the hand, and goes three times round the pit, and at each round makes a hole in the pot; and when these three rounds are done breaks the pot, which is small, and throws the torch into the pit. Then they apply the fire, and when the body is burned comes the wife with all the feasters and washes her feet, and then a Brāhman performs over her certain ceremonies according to their law; and when he has finished doing this, she draws off with her own hand all the jewels that she wears, and divides them among her female relatives, and if she has sons she commends them to her most honoured relatives. When they have taken off all she has on, even her good clothes, they put on her some common yellow cloths, and her relatives take her hand and she takes a branch in the other, and goes singing and running to the pit where the fire is, and then mounts on some steps which are made high up by the pit. Before they do this they go up three times round the fire, and then she mounts the steps and holds in front of her a mat that prevents her from seeing the fire. They throw into the fire a cloth containing rice, and another in which they carry betel leaves, and her comb and mirror with which she adorned herself, saying that all these are needed to adorn herself by her husband's side. Finally she takes leave of all, and puts a pot of oil on her head, and casts herself into the fire with such courage that it is a thing of wonder; and as soon as she throws herself in, the relatives are ready with firewood and quickly cover her with it, and after this is done they all raise loud lamentations. When a captain dies, however many wives he has they all burn themselves, and when the King dies they do the same." The above description of a sati is so graphic that we may feel quite sure that Nuniz actually witnessed one of these ghastly performances.

The spot where these cremations took place was in all probability, at Nimbāpuram close to Talarigattu [see the Map] where there is a large cinder mound covered over with rank vegetation and trees of considerable age. This mound is composed of alternate layers of slag-like cinders and ashy earth mixed with small fragments of calcined bone and there is no doubt that it represents the remains of those slain in battle, or else the recognized sati ground of the old city. It will be noticed that Nuniz states "at the place where they are always burned," thus indicating a spot specially set aside for this purpose. He also informs us that the widow went to the sati ground on horseback, so we may presume that the sati took place a mile or two outside the city. The local explanation of the presence of this great mound of cinders at Nimbāpuram, is that it represents the cremated remains of the great Vāli who was slain by Rāma as related above and the mound is regarded as sacred in consequence.

The doctrine of transmigration of souls and the custom of cremating the dead and casting the ashes on the waters of a sacred river or tank did not encourage tomb building. The Muhammadans on the other hand, who made tomb building such a special feature of their religion, have left us a few monuments of this kind outside the city but they are not of much architectural importance. The best examples are at Kadirampuram and are illustrated in Fig. 69.

Tulāpurusha-dāna Ceremony.

Situated at a short distance to the south-west of the Vitthala temple [see the Map] is the curious monument illustrated in Fig. 13. It has been named the "King's Balance"

FIG. 13.—THE KING'S BALANCE.

for the sake of brevity and convenience, but its correct name is the *Tulāpurusha-dāna* Monument, that is, the monument on which the kings on certain special occasions, such as a coronation, the day of a lunar or solar eclipse, a new-moon, or New Year's Day, performed the quaint religious ceremony of having themselves weighed against their own weight in gold or precious stones which were afterwards distributed among the Brāhmans.

Supported on two lofty granite pillars of elegant appearance, is a massive stone beam or transom designed like the waggon-headed roofs of the temple gateways or *gopurams.* On the underside of the transom are carved three stone rings for the support of the large pair of scales, which were fixed to the beam whenever the ceremony was performed. The monument faces the east, and, on this side, the base of one of the stone pillars is ornamented with a crude sculptural representation of a king and his two wives. Early Indian and Sinhalese kings followed this strange custom on their coronation, and the Vijayanagar sovereigns, too, as we learn from some of their inscriptions, made this gift in accordance with the rules laid down in the *sāstrās.* One inscription records that, after the capture of the famous Hill Fort at Kondavidu in the Guntūr district on the 23rd June 1515 A.D., Krishna Rāya, the greatest of all the Vijayanagar sovereigns, in the same year, accompanied by his two wives, Chinnadēvi-Amma and Tirumaladēvi-Amma [see Fig. 14] who appear to have accompanied him during his military campaigns visited the temple of Amarēsvara near Dharanikota (the historic Dhannayakataka), bestowed there the munificent gift known as Tulāpurusha-dāna, Ratnadhēnu, and Saptasagara and presented some villages to the temple.* In all probability, the sculptured representation of a king and his two queens carved on the base of the pillar mentioned above, is intended to represent Krishna Rāya and his two wives referred to in the inscription. Achyuta-Rāya (A.D. 1530—1542), who succeeded Krishna Rāya was most profuse in his gifts to temples and Brāhmans. One inscription, which is registered in the Annual Report of the Assistant Superintendent for Epigraphy,† records that on one occasion when Achyuta Rāya performed the *Tulāpurusha-dāna* ceremony, he "weighed himself against pearls."

In the *Dānasāgara,* an early work of about the eleventh century of the Christian era, it is stated "that the ceremony of *Tulāpurusha-dāna* must be performed on auspicious occasions

---

* A.S.R., 1908–09, p. 178. † 1899–1900, p. 29.

such as the day of equinox, solstices, the end or beginning of a *yuga*, the day of a lunar or solar eclipse, *sankrānti*, or

FIG. 14.—METAL IMAGES OF KRISHNA RĀYA AND HIS TWO QUEENS, TIRUPATI TEMPLE, CHITTOOR DISTRICT.

new-moon." The places for the ceremony, according to the same authority, "must be sacred places of pilgrimage, a temple, a garden, a cow-pen, a house, a forest, or the neighbourhood of a river's bank. The images of Brahma, Śiva and Achyuta (Vishnu) must be worshipped. A golden figure representing Vāsudēva must be placed in the centre of the beam. Four Brāhmans, versed severally in the four Vedas, must be placed in the four different quarters, north, south, east and west, respectively. These will perform *homa* to propitiate the lords of the eight regions, the Lokapālas. The donor must put on all his ornaments, hold his sword and wear his armour, and sit in the scale looking peacefully at the image of Vāsudēva. After the weighing is over the gold coins are to be distributed among Brāhmans." For, as the same authority states, "a wise man must not keep in his house the money thus allotted, for a long time. He who weighs against his own person in gold and distributes it among Brāhmans will extricate his forefathers from ten generations (past and present) and from all misery."

A few years ago, the Maharaja of Travancore performed the *Tulāpurusha-dāna* ceremony; so this quaint old custom still survives in some parts of India, and no doubt the Brāhmans would feel sorry to see a custom so advantageous to themselves disappear.

PART II.

THE BUILDINGS DESCRIBED

FORTIFICATIONS AND IRRIGATION WORKS.

With the exception of their vast extent, their massive construction and the ingenuity with which the natural advantages of the country have been utilized, the fortifications present few points of interest. With the perennial Tungabhadra, unfordable for many miles, on its northern boundary and the almost unclimbable rocky hills, linked together by these long lines of massive walls on its other sides, the city was a place of great strength in the then conditions of warfare. The gateways in the walls are mostly small openings spanned by stone lintels supported from below by corbels in the usual Hindu style of construction, but one or two of them are more ornamental. The road which leads northwards to the Vitthala temple passes under one of these latter [see Fig. 15]. The remains of the brick and plaster turret above this gateway is built in the Indo-Saracenic style, while the lower portion is constructed of stone in the usual Hindu manner. In all probability, the gateway was repaired or improved by some of the Muhammadan soldiers serving as mercenaries under the Vijayanagar kings. Another example of a gateway built in this same style is the handsome domed building illustrated in Fig. 16. It is situated at a distance of about half a mile to the north-east of the Pattābhi Rāma temple surrounded by ruined fortifications. It faces the east and appears to have been one of the main entrances on this side of the city. On the inner side of the gateway is a small guard-room containing a large image of the monkey deity Hanumān. Between this gateway and the Gānigitti Jaina temple on the Kampli road, situated about four hundred yards to the south-east of the latter, is Bhima's gateway, so called because it contains a large well-carved bas-relief image of Bhima. It also contains a large inscribed memorial pillar of some kind, but unfortunately, the inscription is no longer legible. It is a handsome gateway as may be seen in Fig. 17,

Gateways.

and the only one existing built in this particular style. It is provided with a sallyport and protected at the sides with massive walls and is the most strongly fortified entrance existing at Vijayanagar.

FIG. 15.—GATEWAY ON THE TALARIGATTU ROAD.

Originally, the different lines of fortifications extended as far as Hospet (Nāgalāpur). Paes describing the entrance into the city from this end, says it was "a very strong city fortified with walls and towers, and the gates at the entrance very strong, with towers at the gates; these walls are not like those of other cities, but are made of very strong masonry such as would be found in few other parts, and inside very beautiful rows of buildings made after their manner with flat roofs."

FIG. 16. DOMED GATEWAY TO THE EAST OF HAMPI.

All traces of these walls at Hospet have disappeared. In the 1866 famine, workers on relief were employed in throwing down much of the fort wall into the moat which then surrounded it, this latter having become a receptacle for all kinds of unsavoury rubbish.

Irrigation Works.

All the early travellers, who visited Vijayanagar before its fall, were struck with astonishment at the wonderful irrigation system that prevailed throughout the city. Thus Nuniz relates:—" This King (Krishna Rāya) also made in his time a

FIG. 17.—BHIMA'S GATEWAY.

lake for water, which lies between two very lofty hills. But since he had no means in the country for making it, nor any one who could do it, he sent to Goa to ask the Governor to send some Portuguese masons, and the Governor sent him João della Ponte, a great worker in stone, to whom the King told how he wanted the tank built. Though it seemed to this man impossible to be made, nevertheless he told the King he would do it and asked him to have lime prepared, at which the King laughed much, for in his country when they build a house they do not understand how to use lime. The King commanded to throw down quantities of stone and cast down many great rocks into the valley, but everything fell to pieces, so that all the work done in the day was destroyed each night and the King amazed at this, sent to call his wise men and sorcerers and asked them what they thought of this thing. They told him that his idols were not pleased with this work, it being so great and he giving them nothing, and that unless he spilled there the blood of men or women or buffaloes that the work would never be finished. So the King sent to bring hither all the men who were his prisoners, and who deserved death, and ordered them there to be beheaded; and with this the work advanced. He made a bank across the middle of the valley so lofty and wide that it was a crossbow-shot in breadth and length, and had large openings (sluices); and below it he put pipes by which the water escaped, and when they wish so to do they close these. By means of this water they made many improvements in the city, and many channels by which they irrigated rice-fields and gardens, and in order that they might improve their lands he gave the people the lands which are irrigated by this water free for nine years, until they had made their improvements, so that the revenue already amounts to 20,000 *pardaos.*

Above this tank is a very large ridge all enclosed, and in the middle some very strong gates with two towers, one on one side and one on the other; and within are always posted 1,000 men on guard. For through this gate all things must enter that come into the two cities, since in order to enter the city of Bisnaga (Vijayanagar) there is no other road but this, all other roads meeting there." Mr. Sewell commenting on the probable position of this tank states *:— "Both Paes and Nuniz mention this lake, and as the former actually saw it under construction it may have been begun in A.D. 1520. I think that this is the large lake, now dry, to be seen at the north-western mouth of the valley entering into the Sandur hills south-west of Hospet, the huge bank of which has been utilized for the conveyance of the high-road from Hospet to the southern taluks. If so, the fact of its original failure is interesting to us, because for many years past this vast work has been entirely useless. The description given by Nuniz accords with the position of this tank, which was doubtless intended partly for irrigation purposes, and partly for the supply of water to the 'new city,' Nāgalāpur, † the King's favourite residence, now known as Hospet. The chronicler mentions the existence of lofty ridges on each side, strong gates and towers guarding the entrance, and states that this was the principal approach to the capital from the south; all which data coincide with the position of the tank and road in question. It is through these gates that the Portuguese travellers entered Vijayanagar. This view is supported by the account given by Paes. Writing of the approach to Vijayanagar from the western coast, and describing the 'first range,' i.e., the first that is seen on passing upwards from the plains, he states that in these hills was the principal entrance from that side. He alludes to the gates and wall, and the city, Nāgalāpur, constructed by King Krishna. Then he writes 'the King made a tank there,' i.e., close to Hospet, at the mouth of two hills, and in order to do this, 'broke down a hill.' He saw innumerable people at work on the tank. He confirms the story of Nuniz as to the sixty human beings offered in sacrifice to ensure the security of the dam. Both writers are therefore describing the same tank, and taking the chronicles together, I can have no doubt as to the soundness of my identification."

Whether this same tank which furnished the water-supply to Nāgalāpur also supplied the city of Vijayanagar, is not

* "A Forgotten Empire," pp. 162–63.

† Krishna Rāya built the outlying town of Nāgalāpur prior to A.D. 1520 in honour of his favourite wife, the quondam courtesan, Nāgalā Dēvi.

clear from the descriptions given by Paes and Nuniz. If such was the case, then the mean water level of the tank in question must have been at a very considerable elevation above the plains in order to supply the stone aqueduct and existing water channels situated on the high ground near the Throne Platform. The water channels irrigating the low-lying cultivated lands on the northern side of the city, derive their supply from a channel fed by the Tungabhadra river.

The Stone Aqueduct. The lofty position of the stone aqueduct, shown in Fig. 18, suggests that the water-supply to the buildings in the citadel was derived from some tank situated in the higher hills to the north-east of the city, but no such tank exists on this side, so in all probability, the water was obtained from a well outside the citadel in the usual Indian fashion by means of large leather-buckets worked by bullocks, the water being poured into a main channel connected with branch pipes. The existing remains of the stone channel and earthenware pipes show clearly enough, that the chief object of this particular irrigation scheme was for the supply of water to the few small tanks, baths and stone troughs connected with the buildings in the citadel. No attempt was made to supply the whole city with running water from this side of the site. The northern side of the city was, and still is, provided with a continual flow of water carried by the Turuttu irrigation channel, but at no period could the citadel have obtained its water-supply direct from the river owing to its greater elevation above the latter. The amount of water required to fill the tanks and baths belonging to the State Apartments would no doubt be large, but not sufficiently so, to make the supply by wells and manual labour impossible, especially in a city where the cost of labour would not be considered so far as the King and his household were concerned. Stone aqueducts similar in all respects to the one shown in Fig. 18, connected with wells and used for irrigation purposes, may still be seen in working order in a few places in the Madras Presidency. It is probable that the water-supply to the citadel was obtained by this means and not by water carried in channels or pipes from the tank described by Paes and Nuniz which was situated at a distance of at least ten miles from the citadel. If one follows the stone aqueduct near

Fig. 18.—Stone Water Channel near the Throne Platform.

the Throne Platform in an easterly direction, it will be found to lead straight up to the enclosure walls of the citadel on this side. Here, will be found a double line of enclosure walls, separated by a deep roadway about 10 yards in width. Apparently the aqueduct was carried over these two walls as it is continued on the other side and runs due east in the direction of the Chandra Sēkara temple. At this point, one line of the channel appears to run towards the Zenānā Enclosure and also to the Octagonal Bath to the north-east, and the other runs parallel to the western enclosure wall of the Chandra Sēkara temple and thence to a small ruined square masonry tower which stands half-way between this temple and the Queen's Bath. From this tower, the channel led to the Queen's Bath. To the south of this tower, standing alongside of the road to Hampi and overlooking the ramparts, is a large mound of earth and ruined masonry, evidently the remains of a lofty platform, or an inclined ramp. Standing on this mound and facing the south, a large masonry-lined well will be seen in the field just below the ramparts and within a fifty yards of the mound. In all probability, the water was raised from this well and carried by a channel to a small tank or cistern at the foot of the ramparts, immediately below the mound above. It was then apparently raised to the level of the ramp by the usual means of leather-buckets worked by bullocks and thence carried across the road by an aqueduct to a masonry built cistern located on the top of the tower opposite. At this point, the water was apparently allowed to descend by means of a closed channel or pipes, into the two main channels mentioned above.

No wells could have been sunk on the high ground to the north of the Queen's Bath, as the ground there is nothing but sheet rock below the surface. It was no doubt the presence of the higher level at this particular spot which necessitated the channel supplying the citadel being led along the lower ground outside the Chandra Sēkara temple so as to avoid this rising ground. Providing the platform on the ramparts and the water-tower were of sufficient elevation, there would have been no difficulty in carrying a supply of water by means of a closed channel into the citadel in the manner suggested above.

Large Stone Trough.

This great trough stands in the enclosure in front of the large ruined basement of the King's Audience Hall which faces the north. This open space appears to have been the courtyard in which those desiring an audience with the King waited for an interview. The stone trough would be necessary for the supply of water to the horses and elephants belonging to ambassadors, nobles and others, seeking an audience with the King. It is carved out of a single block of granite measuring 41½ feet in length, 3 feet in width, and 2 feet 9 inches in thickness. It is provided with a small drainage hole at one end for flushing out purposes. Fig. 19 gives one a good idea of its vast proportions.

The Queen's Bath.

This is a square building in the Indo-Saracenic style of architecture and is one of the first buildings the visitor meets with on approaching the buildings in the citadel from Kāmalāpur. Outside, it is a particularly plain and uninteresting structure surrounded by a narrow moat. In the centre of the building is a small tank, or swimming bath. Around this is an arched corridor with small projecting balconies overlooking the bath in the centre. The walls and arches contain some pretty stucco work here and there, similar in style to that adorning the Lotus Mahal in the Zenānā Enclosure, the two buildings being obviously of the same period. There is no direct evidence that this building was used as the Queen's Bath, and it is situated at a distance of half a mile from the Zenānā buildings. However, both ornamental baths and gardens belonging to the royal household were often situated at a considerable distance from the palace buildings and were used as pleasure resorts by the King and the ladies of the Zenānā.

Octagonal Pavilion.

About a quarter of a mile from the Queen's Bath as one proceeds in a north-westerly direction along the main road to Hampi, may be seen a large eight-sided structure standing by the roadside. Like the Queen's Bath, it is built in the Indo-Saracenic style and evidently belongs to the same period. It has arched openings on all sides and contains a little fountain-basin in the centre and a massive stone trough carved out of a single block of stone, which is said to have been kept full of milk for distribution to the poor during the big festivals. The remains of the old earthenware water-pipes

Fig. 19.—Stone Trough, facing the King's Audience Hall.

which supplied the little fountain with water may be seen close by. The building is not of much architectural value but it is of interest and a somewhat uncommon structure illustrating how these great Vijayanagar princes thought of their poorer subjects. On the opposite side of the road situated in a field may be seen the remains of another stone water channel with a number of stone slabs on each side of it provided with plate and dish-like depressions carved upon them for the use of pilgrims when preparing and taking their food. In this case, the water-supply was, in all probability, obtained direct from some well in the immediate neighbourhood. This same channel also supplied the building just described.

At a short distance to the north of the Chandra Sēkara temple is a well-built eight-sided tank with the remains of a little pavilion in the centre and an open pillared corridor with a flat roof running all round the bath. Like the Queen's Bath, it appears to have been used as a pleasure resort and probably dates from the same period. **Octagonal Bath.**

There is also a large masonry-lined tank of the usual type of Hindu construction situated on the left-hand side of the road as one enters the citadel from Kāmalāpur. This is the largest tank in the citadel and may have been used as a swimming bath and for aquatic sports. It obtained its water-supply from the stone channel mentioned above.

The visitor to Hampi crosses this irrigation channel just before arriving at the Krishna temple on the main road to Hampi from Kāmalāpur. The name means "swift" and is certainly deserved. The channel takes off from the Turuttu anicut across the Tungabhadra about a mile west of Hampi and is a most remarkable work, running for miles often through solid rock, along the foot of the hills. It was perhaps made by Bukka II (fourteenth century) and it now waters most of the wet lands which wind in and out about the ruins, its supply being supplemented by the tank at Kāmalāpur. **The Turutti Channel.**

BUILDINGS IN THE CITADEL.

Just north-east of the Queen's Bath and inside the line of walls around the citadel, are still standing a few yards of one of the stone aqueducts described above and mentioned by **Throne Platform.**

Abdur Razzāk. "One sees," he said, "numerous running streams and canals formed of chiselled stone, polished and smooth." Immediately north of it rise the striking ruins of the Throne Platform, or the "House of Victory," as Paes calls it. The people know it now as the Dasara Dibba or Mahānavami Dibba, meaning the platform (dibba) used during the nine days' festival called variously the Dasara, the Mahānavami, or the Navarātri (nine nights). Paes says it was called the House of Victory because it was built by Krishna Dēva Rāya on his return from his victorious campaign against the King of Orissa.(A.D. 1513) and his description of the festivities at the Dasara, of which this building was, throughout the centre, is one of the most vivid parts of his chronicle.

There are a considerable number of these stone platforms or basements of buildings among the ruins in the citadel, but none can compare with this one in height or beauty [Fig. 20]. It is a very massive structure, originally faced with carved granite blocks and slabs which have subsequently been partly refaced with dark green chlorite stone on the front or west side of the platform. Half-way up, there is a terraced walk around the structure, and on the upper floor on the east side, there is a small room below the level of the floor, approached by a narrow flight of stone steps on each side of the chamber.* The spaces between the different rows of the plinth mouldings of the platform are most elaborately carved in a similar style to that employed in the ornamentation of the enclosure walls of the Hazāra Rāma temple, the different scenes representing processions of soldiers, horses, elephants, camels and dancing-girls. Whilst other bas-reliefs depict hunting scenes and conventional animals. Owing to the nature of granite, these sculptures are necessarily somewhat crude in execution but they are nevertheless intensely interesting. The later sculptures, executed in chlorite stone, are more highly and beautifully finished, and are perhaps the best sculptural antiquities that survive here. From the remains found on top of some of these stone basements, there

* It is possible that the wonderful throne of gold and gems used only during the Dasara celebration, was kept in this small room.

A.H.L.

FIG. 20.—THRONE PLATFORM FROM THE SOUTH.

is no doubt that the superstructures were constructed in brick and plaster with carved wooden pillars supporting timber-framed roofs, probably covered with small copper plates like the roofs of the temples on the West Coast. In this manner, some of the original buildings may have been of several storeys and of great height. This was evidently the case with the "King's Audience Hall" which, according to Abdur Razzāk, "was elevated above all the rest of the lofty buildings in the citadel." There can be little doubt that this platform represents the remains of the magnificent pavilion in which was placed the wonderful royal throne of gold and gems used by the sovereign during the Mahānavami or great nine days' festival held in the autumn every year when all the chiefs, nobles, and captains had to assemble at Vijayanagar to pay their rents and do homage to the King. Nuniz describes this festival as follows *:—"This takes place in the month of September when for nine days they make great feasts. Some say that they do this in honour of the nine months during which Our Lady bore her Son in the womb; others say that it is only done because at this time the captains come to pay their rents to the King, which feasts are conducted in the following manner:—

The first day they put nine castles in a piece of ground which is in front of the palace, which castles are made by the nine principal captains in the kingdom. They are very lofty and are hung with rich cloths, and in them are many dancing-girls and also many kinds of contrivances. Besides these nine, every captain is obliged to make each one his castle, and they come to show these to the King. Each one has his separate device, and they all come like this during the nine days of the feast. The officers of the city are bound to come with their devices each day at night, just as in our festivals, and in these nine days they slaughter animals and make sacrifice. The first day they kill nine male buffaloes and nine sheep and nine goats, and thenceforward they kill each day more, always doubling the number; and when they have finished slaying these beasts, there come nine horses and nine

---

* The descript'on given by Nuniz relates how this festival took place in the reign of Achyuta Rāya (A.D. 1530—1542).

elephants of the King, and these come before the King covered with flowers—roses—and with rich trappings. Before them goes the Chief Master of the Horse with many attendants, and they make salaam to the King. And when these have finished making their salaams there come from within priests, and they bring rice and other cooked edibles and water, and fire, and many kinds of scents, and they offer prayers and throw the water over the horses and elephants, just (as our priests do with) holy water; and they put chaplets of roses on them. This is done in the presence of the King, who remains seated on a throne of gold and precious stones; he never sits on this except only this once in the year. And the King that now reigns does not sit on it, for they say that whoever sits on it must be a very truthful man, one who speaks the whole truth, and this king never does so.* Whilst this is going on there pass by the King fully a thousand women, dancing and posturing before him. After all the devices that have been prepared have been witnessed all the horses of the King pass by, covered with their silken trappings, and with much adornment of gold and precious stones on their heads, and then all the elephants and yokes of oxen † in the middle of the arena in front of the palace. After these have been seen there come thirty-six of the most beautiful of the King's wives covered with gold and pearls, and much work of seed-pearls, and in the hands of each a vessel of gold with a lamp of oil burning in it; and with these women come all the female servants and the other wives of the King, with canes in their hands tipped with gold and with torches burning; and these then retire inside with the King. These women are so richly bedecked with gold and precious stones that they are hardly able to move.

In this way during these nine days they are compelled to search for all things which will give pleasure to the King.

The King has a thousand wrestlers for these feasts who wrestle before the King, but not in our manner, for they strike

---

* Achyuta Rāya.

† Mr. Sewell states that the meaning here is doubtful, but he thinks that in all probability yokes of oxen are referred to. During the big festivals these are often handsomely decorated. Camels, too, appeared at some of these festivals as may be seen from the bas-relief sculptures on the Throne platform.

and wound each other with two circlets with points which they carry in their hands to strike with, and the one most wounded goes and takes his reward in the shape of a silk cloth, such as the King gives to these wrestlers. They have a captain over them, and they do not perform any other service in the kingdom. And after these nine days are finished the Rao (King) rides out and goes to hold a review of the troops of his captains. Within these nine days the King is paid all the rents that he receives from his kingdom; for, as already said, all the land belongs to the King, and from his hand the captains held it."

Many of the scenes described by Nuniz and other early travellers are depicted in the bas-relief sculptures adorning the walls of this platform. Some of the most interesting sculptures will be found on the south side of the platform. Fig. 21 shows some of the details of the bas-reliefs on the east retaining wall of the steps on this side. The upper course of stone is decorated with a procession of elephants. Two foreign-looking men with pointed beards and Persian-like caps are shown bowing to a group of figures seated on a throne. Perhaps the scene is intended to represent a visit of two foreign ambassadors to the court. There is a pronounced Jaina style about all these older bas-reliefs, and, at times, it is a little difficult to know whether some of the figures represent men or women owing to the curious manner in which both sexes wear their hair. Even at the present day on the West Coast, both Jaina and Hindu men may be seen wearing their long hair in a great chignon—like the figures portrayed in these sculptures. Curiously enough, one of the earliest inscribed Vijayanagar records is a sculptured piece of stone discovered by Mr. Sewell in July 1893, on the north-west side of this platform. This inscription records the death of a Jaina teacher named Maladhāri-Dēva who may be identical with Mallishēna Maladhāri-Dēva of Sravana Belgola in Mysore (A.D. 1129).*

Below the elephant procession, we have a flat band or fillet ornamented with sacred geese and conventional crocodiles, a favourite design of the early Jains and Buddhists. Then comes a dado decorated with three rows of dancing-girls and

* Vide *Epigraphia Indica*, Vol. III, p. 188.

female musicians, "dancing and posturing before the King" as Nuniz has it. Although as a work of art, the sculpture is

FIG. 21.—DETAILS OF SCULPTURES ON THE EAST WALL OF THE STEPS ON THE SOUTH SIDE OF THE THRONE PLATFORM.

poor, the figures are not lacking in spirit and action. The plinth is decorated in a similar manner to the fillet above the dado. Perhaps, nowhere is the Jaina influence more marked than in the bas-reliefs shown in Fig. 22, these sculptures are situated to the left-hand side of those just described. In the top panel we have a representation of a parade of the King's horses. Next comes a hunting scene. One man is shown

FIG. 22.—DETAILS OF SCULPTURES ON THE SOUTH WALL OF THE THRONE PLATFORM.

spearing a tiger or panther, whilst two men, one armed with a bow, and the other with a curiously shaped weapon and leading brace of greyhounds, are depicted hunting antelope.

In the centre is a tree in which are two armed men being attacked by some wild beast. Below the tree is a boar on one side and a cross on the other, the latter is certainly peculiar, but in this case it is merely a conventional method of representing an ornamental tank. Below, are represented two boxers giving an exhibition of the "noble art" before the King in the manner related by Nuniz. To the left, we have a very Assyrian-looking bas-relief, representing a warrior slaying a bear by calmly plunging a dagger into its open mouth as it charges. The warriors who represent nobles or captains and the King are portrayed wearing their hair in the Jaina style mentioned above, but the boxers and the greyhound slipper are shown with short hair. So, perhaps, only the nobles were permitted to wear their hair in this peculiarly feminine manner. One finds the same kind of warrior sculptured on the sati memorials as may be seen in Fig. 11. Processions of horses and warriors, camels, carrying drummers with kettle drums shaped like baskets [see Fig. 23], elephants, dancing-girls and musicians make up the rest of the scenes depicted in these quaint old bas-reliefs. The sculptors have tried to represent the gorgeous processions and sports which took place at the Mahānavami festival around this Throne Platform and which have been so graphically described by the early European travellers who visited this wonderful city when it was in its full glory and splendour. Another festival mentioned by these travellers, and one which is actually depicted here, is the "Holi Festival." Thus Nicolo states :— "There are also three other festival days, during which they sprinkle all passers-by, even the King and Queen themselves with saffron water, placed for that purpose by the wayside. This is received by all with much laughter." The sculpture, shown in Fig. 24, is situated on the left-hand side of the steps leading up to the top of the platform on the front or west side, and shows a young noble taking part in this festival with a group of dancing-girls, two of the latter being armed with squirts full of saffron water. Here and there, may be seen some well-carved figures and animals among these later and more highly finished sculptures on this side of the platform, some of the mouldings too, are particularly beautiful, but unfortunately, most of the work has been damaged, probably by Muhammadan soldiers after the disastrous battle of Talikōta.

FIG. 23.—SCULPTURES ON THE SOUTH WALL OF THE THRONE PLATFORM.

A charming view of the ruins in the citadel may be obtained from the top of this platform, the Zenānā Enclosure with its two lofty Watch Towers, the Elephant Stables standing alongside of it, the Hazāra Rāma temple, and the Danaik's Enclosure may all be clearly seen from here, whilst granite peaks and rocks, tors and logging-stones indent the horizon in picturesque confusion.

Lying on the ground close under the northern wall of the platform, and formerly hidden from view by debris and bushes, was discovered the huge stone door now set up by the **Stone Door**

FIG. 24.—SCULPTURE REPRESENTING THE HOLI FESTIVAL, THRONE PLATFORM.

roadside on this side of the Throne Platform. It is a remarkable piece of work, cut (bolt-sockets and all) from a single stone, and panelled to represent a battened wooden door. There is nothing to indicate to which building it originally belonged.

Basement of a Palace. At a short distance to the west of the Throne Platform is another large and ornamental basement of a ruined building. Presumably, it represents the ruins of a palace, possibly, that of the King since it is situated in the royal enclosure close to the Throne Platform and the King's Audience Hall to the north of it. The basements of some of the temples and palaces are often ornamented in the same way, by processions of horses, elephants and dancing-girls, but in the case of the former, the walls of the superstructure are invariably built of stone up to the first cornice, whereas the walls of the palaces were built of brick and plaster with wooden pillars carrying the upper storeys and the roof. When the debris and bushes were removed from this basement at the time when it was excavated, the remains of brick and plaster walls were found standing on the top of the platform together with a quantity of wood ash showing that the superstructure had been burned down and collapsed on to its basement below. This basement is about five feet in height and the main entrance faced the north. Had it been a temple the entrance would in all probability have faced the east. The basement is divided into long panels representing the usual Dasara processions with alternate rows of richly carved arabesque and lotus leaf mouldings in between. It is a handsome platform and one well worth the trouble and expense of unearthing it.

Underground Chamber. This curious little structure is situated close to the last mentioned building. There seems little doubt that, originally, this chamber was an underground shrine or private chapel provided with a procession path around the main shrine. It is square on plan with a doorway facing the east, which opens into a little gloomy passage for circumambulation which was approached from the ground above by a narrow passage and a short flight of steps on its northern side. The stone bases of four pillars show that the roof was originally formed of stone slabs resting on beams. The passage is constructed in the same manner, and the whole of the interior was originally plastered and whitewashed. From the broken slabs, stone beams and mouldings removed from the interior of the building during repairs, it is clear that this little shrine originally had a superstructure built above it, which collapsed and fell

FIG. 25.—KING'S AUDIENCE HALL.

into the underground chamber below, breaking the roof over the shrine in the process. In order to prevent accident and to keep out surface water and rubbish from collecting in the interior, a modern dwarf parapet wall has been constructed around the opening.

The King's Audience Hall. At a distance of about fifty yards to the north of the Underground Chamber is the large platform illustrated in Fig. 25. It is the largest basement of a building among the ruins and was undoubtedly a building of considerable importance. The main entrance faced the north and on this side there was once an open courtyard in front of the building. An examination of the upper surface of the platform shows that originally there were no less than six rows of pillars each row containing ten pillars, as may be seen from the existing stone bases let into the floor of the platform. When the debris was removed from the top of this platform no remains of the pillars were found, so we may conclude that these were of timber and, in all probability, carved, painted and gilded. The mouldings of the base are plain and simple and not elaborately carved like those of the palaces and some of the larger temples. The south and west sides of the building were closed with rubble masonry walls, and, apparently, there was once a stone staircase leading up to the upper storeys of the building on the south side. As already stated above, Abdur Razzāk informs us that "the King's Audience Hall was elevated above all the rest of the lofty buildings in the citadel." It was obviously, originally a very large and many-pillared Darbar Hall with one or more storeys above it, mainly constructed in timber. In all probability it was burned down to its stone basement by the Muhammadans. Standing in the courtyard facing the platform is the large stone trough already referred to.

The Mint. On the south-west side of the King's Audience Hall is a large walled enclosure which is generally said to represent the ruins of the Royal Mint. Judging from the complete manner in which the Muhammadans have obliterated all traces of the buildings it once contained, this conjecture is probably correct. On leaving the courtyard in front of the King's Audience Hall, one passes through two gateways on the northern side of the citadel to the wonderful temple of Hazāra Rāma or Rāmachandra.

Hazāra Rāma Temple.

This temple is generally supposed to have been the private place of worship of the kings. Its particularly ornate character and its close proximity to the royal enclosure seems to favour this supposition. Like the Throne Platform, it was begun (as the inscriptions within testify) by the great Krishna Dēva Rāya in 1513 * and the outer surfaces of its enclosure walls are covered with bas-reliefs very similar to those on that building.

Although a comparatively small building, it is one of the most perfect specimens of Hindu temple architecture of the Vijayanagar period in existence. The temple, together with its attendant Amman shrine, stands in a walled enclosure measuring 110 feet from north to south and 200 feet from east to west, and faces the east [see Fig. 26]. It was dedicated to Rāma or Rāmachandra, one of the ten incarnations of Vishnu, and the bas-reliefs adorning the walls and pillars of the two shrines and on the inner surface of the courtyard walls, depict the main incidents in the Rāmāyana with a few scenes from the Mahābhārata. In order to understand and appreciate these wonderful bas-reliefs at their true value, it is essential that the visitor to Hampi be familiar with the main outlines of the legends of Rāma and Krishna as related above in *Part I.*

The temple is provided with a handsome porch in front which leads into a central hall, the roof of which is mainly supported by four particularly beautiful and highly polished black stone pillars, richly carved and crowned with bracket capitals of Indo-Corinthian appearance. One of these pillars is illustrated in Fig. 27. Although a Vaishnava temple, several Saivite figures appear on these and other pillars in this temple, thus showing a great absence of bigotry. The north-east pillar contains a bas-relief of Vishnu riding on a

* One inscription records that he gave six tax-free villages to the god Ramachandra Dēva in Saka 1435 (A.D. 1513), on the occasion of a solar eclipse for the merit of his parents. Another inscription in the same temple registers the construction of a tank in A.D. 1520 at the village of Tārūr in Sondur-rājya. This village was granted to the Rāmachandra temple by Krishna Rāya in A.D. 1513.

FIG. 26. HAZĀRA RĀMA TEMPLE, SOUTH-WEST VIEW.

horse which is apparently intended to represent Kalki, the tenth and last incarnation yet to come, in which Vishnu will appear on a white horse with a drawn sword, to restore the

FIG. 27.—CARVED BLACKSTONE PILLAR IN THE HAZĀRA RĀMA TEMPLE.

order of righteousness. The Buddha incarnation of Vishnu is also shown in two bas-reliefs on the exterior surface of the sanctum walls of this temple.

The north and south sides of the main hall open out into pillared side porches with steps leading out into the court-yard, whilst an entrance on the west side leads into the sanctum or shrine chamber. In here was originally enshrined an image of Vishnu in the form of Rāmachandra. The whole of the building, up to the cornice with the massive projecting dripstones, is built of granite, whilst the '*stūpi*' or ornamental tower over the sanctum, and the ruined parapet wall above the flat roof over the central hall and side porches, is built of brick and plaster decorated with stucco figures. This brick and plaster work is now in a very decayed condition but sufficient remains to show how ornamental this portion of the building must have been when complete. Originally, the stucco figures and decorative features of the plaster work were picked out in bright colours partly for the sake of producing a brilliant effect, and partly with a view to representing in an anthropomorphic manner the different incarnations and legends connected with the deity enshrined in the temple.

The exterior walls of the shrine chamber and the pillared porticoes are decorated in a similar manner and with the same object in view, but, here, the bas-reliefs are executed in granite. Besides these interesting bas-reliefs, the beautiful little pilasters and engaged columns, the ornamental niches for detached sculpture, and the handsome mouldings and massive cornices adorning the exterior walls of these vo temples are worthy of notice. The double cornice with its heavy projecting dripstones is both beautiful and interesting. The treatment of the underside of the dripstones shows an unmistakable wooden origin for this type of cornice. The curved brackets that would be required to support a projecting wooden cornice of this pattern have all been laboriously reproduced here in stone without any additional support or constructional advantage having been gained in the process. These massive dripstones are only kept in position by being tightly wedged in between the double cornice, the upper cornice being in reality an ornamental and very heavy stone blocking-course, sometimes surmounted with a brick parapet wall in order to increase the weight above so as to prevent the dripstones below from slipping out of position. Such a faulty piece of building construction as this, could only be due to the builders attempting to reproduce in stone, a form which they were perfectly familiar with in

FIG. 28.—DETAILS OF CARVED STONEWORK ON THE AMMAN SHRINE, HAZÁRA RÁMA TEMPLE.

wood, but one which does not lend itself successfully to construction in the former material. The dripstones adorning the Amman shrine and some of the mouldings on the base of the same building show clearly enough that some of the stone carving was copied from metal work. The treatment of the dripstones as may be seen in Fig. 28 shows that the stone mason took, as his model, a curved bracketed wooden cornice covered with thin corrugated metal plates decorated at the angles with embossed brass or copper ornaments. Whilst one of the most beautiful of the base mouldings represents a design composed of a row of metal bracelets like those worn by the dancing-girls of the temples. We know from the remains discovered on some of the ruined stone basements of palaces and other ornamental buildings here, and also from the graphic descriptions recorded by early travellers who visited Vijayanagar in its palmy days, that the superstructures of the chief buildings, other than temples, were mainly constructed in wood, probably elaborately carved in much the same style as that which we now see on the ruined stone temples. The roofs and verandahs were no doubt covered with thin copper sheets or plates to protect the woodwork below. Roofs of this type of construction may still be seen on some of the Jaina temples in South Canara, as at Mudabidri and Karkal. Small wooden mandapas or pavilions with carved bracketed cornices of the same type as that represented in these dripstones may be seen in some of the great temples at Madura, Chidambaram and elsewhere. Owing to the perishable nature of wood, even when protected with a thin metal covering, and the fact that the Muhammadan soldiers set fire to every building that they thought might be destroyed in that manner, it is not surprising that none of these wooden superstructures survive. However, a study of the details shown in some of the existing stone buildings helps one to form a fairly accurate idea of what some of these gorgeous wooden buildings must have appeared like with their painted wood carvings and gilded metal work.

The Amman shrine stands on the north side of the main temple and faces the east. In Southern India, almost every large and important temple dedicated to a male deity is provided with an Amman shrine, in which is placed an image of the goddess who represents the god's consort. Thus a Śiva temple would have an attendant shrine containing an image of the goddess Pārvati, the wife of Śiva; whilst a Vaishnava temple like the one we are now considering, would have an Amman temple enshrining an image of Lakshmi, the consort of Vishnu. In addition to the Amman shrine, most large temples are also provided with attendant temples enshrining images of the god's sons, or his particular vahan or vehicle, or, perhaps, some weird idol representing one of the god's wonderful incarnations. Besides these minor shrines for lesser deities, every large temple courtyard is provided with one or more pillared halls or mandapas, specially constructed and often very handsome buildings, in which during the great temple festivals certain ceremonies connected with the idols enshrined in the temples are performed such as the annual marriage ceremony between the god and his consort. Other mandapas are used as places of religious instruction, and the cloisters or pillared verandahs usually found abutting on to the outer walls of the courtyard, are for the use of the priests, and the pilgrims who visit the temple.

The Amman shrine is always smaller than the main temple but sometimes, as in this case, the ornamentation on the former is more elaborate than that on the latter. The two temples are shown standing together in Fig. 26, and in the foreground will be seen the remains of the old stone water channel, which used to supply all the chief buildings in the citadel with water.

The main temple was originally crowned with the usual dome-shaped brick and plaster ornament known in Southern India as the 'stūpi' which was originally surmounted by a gilded metal kalasa or finial like those which still adorn the shrines in the courtyard of the great Pampāpati temple. The Amman shrine is roofed with a heavy waggon-headed brick and plaster ornament resembling the roofs over the temple gateways, or gopurams, as they are usually called, recalling in outline the curious roofs of the Buddhist chaityas or churches. With this exception, the construction and ornamentation of the shrine chambers of both temples is much the same. The Amman shrine is provided with the usual flat-roofed entrance hall in front.

In the north-east corner of the enclosure is the Kalyana mandapa, or pillared hall used during the big festivals connected with the temple. It was evidently built after the outer enclosure walls were carved and finished, with the result that a number of interesting bas-reliefs adorning the outer walls are now hidden from view by the pillars of the mandapa and also by the unsightly but necessary masonry supports erected by the Public Works Department. However, a number of scenes from the Rāmāyana can still be recognized on these walls. Rāma is shown slaying Tātakī, a demoness who infested the forest through which he was journeying; Jatāyu, the king of the kites, who tried to hinder Rāvana from carrying off Sita and was slain in the attempt, is seen falling to the earth; three men are depicted staggering under the weight of Śiva's bow, which Rāma had to bend to win Sita as his bride; Hanumān is there, interviewing Rāvana in Lanka and sitting on the tip of his curled-up tail in order to make himself as tall as that ten-headed demon; Rāma is shooting his arrow through seven trees at once, to prove to Sugriva that he is a warrior worthy to be trusted; Rāma, Lakshmana and Sita are being ferried across the Ganges; and Rāvana is depicted in his death agony. The whole series is, perhaps, the most noteworthy thing of its kind in the ruins. On the outside of the courtyard, these same walls are decorated with five rows of bas-relief sculpture depicting scenes from the Mahānavami festival, as may be seen in Fig. 29. The top row of the bas-reliefs contains a few scenes from the legend of Krishna and a host of dancing-girls. The second row represents a procession of dancing-girls and female musicians; the third row, a procession of soldiers; the fourth row, a procession of the King's horses; the fifth row, a procession of the State elephants.

The handsome gateway of the courtyard has been left unfinished, otherwise it would have been adorned by a lofty brick and plaster tower of the usual kind. In the verandah on the south side of the enclosure are a number of broken and mutilated sculptures executed in a similar kind of chlorite stone to that used in refacing the Throne Platform. This kind of stone, which is much softer, takes a high polish and is far easier to work than granite, appears to have been chiefly used for the carved images of the gods enshrined in the more important temples. This green stone is not native to the city and must have been quarried elsewhere. Nearly all the buildings are constructed of the pinkish grey granite of the local hills and it is probably the coarse grain of this which led the sculptors to import a more suitable stone from a distance when preparing images of special importance. Although these images are hopelessly ruined, they still show

FIG. 29.—BAS-RELIEFS ON THE OUTER ENCLOSURE WALLS OF THE HAZÁRA RÁMA TEMPLE.

plenty of signs of having been once beautifully finished and highly polished, resembling bronze rather than stone.

Lying in the temple courtyard are a few huge blocks of stone decorated with ornamental battlements. Had the enclosure walls been finished, the coping would have been decorated with a line of battlements carved in this peculiar manner.

INDO-SARACENIC BUILDINGS.

The Zenānā Enclosure.

At a short distance to the north of the Hazāra Rāma temple is a large high-walled enclosure containing the Zenānā buildings. All of these, excepting the small gateways in the enclosure walls, are built in the Indo-Saracenic style of architecture. The construction of the enclosure walls is peculiar, the walls diminish in thickness as the height increases until the coping is reached, the latter being built of cement and originally armed with a row of iron spikes all round. Although the masonry is wonderfully well fitted together, the construction is weak and it is obvious that the wall was erected as a screen to ensure privacy within and not for resistance against attack. Originally, there were only three small entrances into this enclosure. The main entrance faces the west and is illustrated in Fig. 30. It is constructed on the usual lintel and corbel principle, a method which the Hindus preferred to employing the arch, although the latter was known to them long before they came in contact with the Muhammadans as the brick arches in the (eighth century A.D.) temples at Bōdh-Gaya and Bhītargaon near Cawnpore conclusively prove. The two small entrances pierced through the walls on the east and south sides of the enclosure were made merely for the convenience of visitors by the Public Works Department some years ago.

The Queen's Palace.

In the centre of the enclosure is the ruined basement of a palace, possibly, the Queen's Palace, since it is the largest building in the enclosure. Abdur Razzāk, particularly states that when the King desired to see the queen or any of the ladies of the Zenānā, that "he sent for them," which seems to indicate that they lived in a separate building to that occupied by the King. In some accounts of Hampi Ruins, this enclosure is described as containing the "Diwān Khana" or public offices of the kingdom. The nature of the construction of the enclosure walls and the style of the buildings themselves, clearly show that this could not have been the case. Everything points in favour of it having been the Zenānā Enclosure. On the north side of the enclosure,

FIG. 30.—MAIN ENTRANCE INTO THE ZENĀNĀ ENCLOSURE.

guarding a small entrance through the walls at its base, is the lofty Watch Tower shown in Fig. 31. On the opposite side, situated in the south-east corner of the enclosure is the Watch Towers.

FIG. 31.—NORTHERN WATCH TOWER, ZENĀNĀ ENCLOSURE.

Watch Tower illustrated in Fig. 32. They have been described as Watch Towers and perhaps they were used partly for that purpose, but their architectural style suggests

FIG. 32. SOUTHERN WATCH TOWER, ZENĀNĀ ENCLOSURE.

that they were used mainly by the ladies of the Zenānā as pleasure resorts where they might safely watch events taking place outside the enclosure without themselves being seen. A flight of steps leads up to the top floors of both towers and the visitor may obtain a delightful view of the surrounding ruins from either of these and, at the same time, be sure of enjoying a cool breeze on the hottest day. On the east side of the enclosure, close to the modern entrance through the walls, is another little building with a tower that overlooks the Elephant Stables. It is picturesque but not important.

The Lotus Mahal. The finest building in the Zenānā Enclosure is the Lotus Mahal which is a fine example of Indo-Saracenic architecture at its best. It is a pretty little pavilion with an upper storey and contains some excellent stucco ornament. To judge from the clumsy manner in which the staircase to the upper storey has been built, one would imagine that it had been added as an afterthought. It looks as though the architect forgot the staircase when preparing the design and had to provide one after the building was completed. The ground floor is raised as usual on a high and ornamental stone basement but with doubly recessed angles which makes the plan of the building peculiar, a feature which, perhaps, gave rise to its singular appellation. This pavilion is open on all sides and provided with massive pillars and arches supporting the room above which is reached by the flight of steps on the north side. The upper room is provided with numerous little windows on all sides, each window originally having little wooden shutters, a feature which we do not find in any other building here, and one which tends to strengthen the conjecture that these buildings do really represent those of the Zenānā. While the pillars and arches are Muhammadan in character, the base, roof, cornice and stucco ornament are Hindu in design. It is an interesting and not unpleasant blending of these two different styles and a fine example of Indo-Saracenic architecture. In the south-west corner of the enclosure is a little pavilion situated in the middle of a small tank or swimming bath. On the east side, close to the main entrance, is a building which in all probability was used as a guard-room, or quarters for the female guards mentioned by the Portuguese travellers. Just outside the enclosure, on the south side, is the small temple of Ranga containing a large stone image of Hanumān some nine feet high.

FIG. 33.—THE LOTUS MAHAL.

The Elephant Stables. These are situated just outside the Zenānā Enclosure, on the eastern side of the latter. With the exception of some of the tops of the domes, this building is almost entirely Muhammadan in character and faces due west. It is a long oblong building containing eleven roomy stalls or rooms with lofty domed roofs, the central stall having a square turret above it, approached by a flight of steps on each side of the stall. It is a dignified and handsome building. There is nothing but local tradition to prove that this building was used as a stable for the State elephants, and if such had been the case, one would have expected to find a few large iron rings or bars embedded in the floors or walls of the stalls for the purpose of chaining the animals thereto. It is a great pity that the central tower is in ruins. In all probability, this was originally crowned with a Hindu stepped tower similar to that surmounting the Lotus Mahal, or the palace at Chandragiri [see Fig. 6].

Guard-room. Close to the Elephant Stables, facing the south is the Gothic-looking building illustrated in Fig. 35. With the exception of the arched verandah in front of the building, it is similar on plan to the quarters for the female guards inside the Zenānā Enclosure. It has sometimes been fancifully called "the Concert Hall" but this is obviously incorrect. Both on plan and in general arrangement the two buildings are identical, the only difference being that the so-called "Concert Hall" is raised higher above the ground, is now roofless over its central portion and is provided in front with a verandah. Both buildings are oblong on plan and have only one entrance which is in front. Around the walls of the interior is a raised platform extending all round, leaving a large oblong open space in the centre. The raised platform in both buildings is divided up into a number of equal spaces with pillars in between carrying arches supporting the vaulted roofs above. It is possible, and extremely probable, that the spaces between these rows of pillars were originally closed with rubble walls so as to form a number of small rooms or cubicles, similar to those which may still be seen in some portions of the ruined Bazaar at Hampi. In fact, in the building in the Zenānā Enclosure, traces of the old mud walls still exist. A lot of the walls were removed when the buildings

FIG. 34.—THE ELEPHANT STABLES.

were cleaned out and repaired by the Public Works Department. The general impression that these two buildings give one, is that they are "dharmasālās" or rest-houses. In other words, quarters for the guards whose duty it was to protect the Zenānā Enclosure. If the Elephant Stables were used as such, this Gothic-looking building, standing alongside of it, may represent the quarters for the men in charge of the elephants. We know from the chronicles of the European travellers, who visited Vijayanagar, that the ladies of the Zenānā were guarded both by female guards and eunuchs. The quarters for the former would naturally be located within the Zenānā Enclosure, and the quarters for the eunuchs or other guards entrusted with the guarding of the entrances would sure to be close at hand. There is nothing about either of these buildings to suggest a "Concert Hall." As a rule, musical entertainments were conducted in the open or under a pavilion like the Lotus Mahal and not in small closed cubicles like those which originally existed in these two buildings.

The Danaik's Enclosure.

The Danaik was the Commander-in-Chief of the troops and the enclosure containing the ruins of his palace and other apartments is situated at a short distance to the west of the Hazāra Rāma temple, the new road from the citadel to Hampi passing the entrance into the enclosure. In the centre of the enclosure is a ruined basement of a building which, we may presume, represents the remains of the Danaik's palace. There are the remains of several other structures in the enclosure but the only buildings of any interest are a large pillared hall or pavilion which appears to have been converted into a mosque, a lofty tower, similar to but smaller than the one in the south-east corner of the Zenānā Enclosure, and a massive stone built Watch Tower in the north-west corner of the enclosure.

We know from Ferishta,* that although the Vijayanagar kings were constantly at war with the Muhammadans, there was apparently no intolerance of the Mussalmans themselves in the city. He relates that Dēva Rāya II built them a mosque there though he explains that the encouragement they received

---

* Scott's Ferishta I, 118.

FIG. 35.—GUARDS' QUARTERS.

was largely due to their superiority as cavalry and bowmen. The only building (existing) which in any way resembles a mosque, is the one in the Danaik's Enclosure. It is a large pillared hall enclosed on three sides with masonry walls which appear to have been added after the main building was completed. The original design appears to have been an open pavilion somewhat similar to the Lotus Mahal and built in the same style. Like the latter, it is built of brick and stone plastered over and originally stood on an ornamental stone basement or platform. The front of the building faces the north and on this side, where the later plaster work has fallen, may be seen the original carved stonework of the basement. This contains sculpture representing human figures, animals, birds and carved mouldings which are certainly not Muhammadan in character. However, it is clear that, subsequently, an attempt was made to cover up and hide this carved work, apparently at the time when the three side walls were added in order to convert the structure into a mosque-like building. But for the fact that the building faces the north there is nothing against the supposition that it does represent a Muhammadan mosque. As it stands at present, its architectural style is mainly Muhammadan and the structure resembles a mosque in most respects, but it is strange that it should face due north. The niches in the back wall are all of the same size and character and there is no central "mihrab," or prayer-niche, indicating the direction of Mecca, one of the indispensable features of the mosque-plan. On the east side of the building are the remains of a retaining wall and a ramp, apparently used in constructing the building. The presence of the ramp indicates that the building was never properly completed.

Muhammadan Watch Tower.

In the north-west corner of the enclosure there is a lofty square stone tower built in the Muhammadan style. It is a particularly massive structure and resembles a bastion more than a watch tower. With the exception of a little chamber in the basement and the narrow stone staircase on the south side, the tower appears to be solid. On top of the tower is a small room divided on the west side into three little chambers on a raised platform. On the north side there appears to have also been a raised platform in front of the large window on this side which corresponds in size to the window on the west side. Below these two windows are massive corbels for supporting projecting balconies in front. From the shape of these windows, the raised platforms in front of them and the particularly massive nature of the corbels and the tower itself, there seems little doubt that guns were mounted on these platforms. The two little chambers on each side of the western window were probably for the watchmen and the storing of ammunition for emergent occasions, the main powder magazine being located in the basement of the tower which is protected on two sides by the fort walls.* The roof is supported with arches and little domes, two of the latter having fallen. It is a very picturesque old ruin and well worth saving from further decay. An illustration of it as it appears from outside the enclosure is given in Fig. 36.

The rest of the buildings at Hampi constructed in the Indo-Saracenic style are those connected with the wonderful irrigation system, such as the Queen's Bath, the Octagonal Pavilion, and the Octagonal Bath; and a few of the gateways already described. It is unlikely that any of the buildings in this style of architecture are earlier than the fifteenth century and in all probability, most of them are about a century later than that date.

BUILDINGS ON THE ROAD TO HAMPI.

The Underground Temple.

On leaving the Danaik's Enclosure, and following the road in a westerly direction, one comes to the so-called Underground Temple close to the junction of this road with the main road to Hampi. The temple is no longer underground as the accumulated silt and rubbish that once buried it has been removed by the Public Works Department. It is a large Siva temple and it was originally, purposely built below the level of the surrounding ground so that the linga might stand surrounded by water. It seems to have been the chief temple connected with Nāga worship, judging from the number of nāgakals (serpent stones) [see Fig. 7] collected in the north-east corner of the temple. The big gateway facing the east

* The entrance into the powder magazine was closed by the Public Works Department when the building was repaired.

FIG. 36.—WATCH TOWER IN THE DANAIK'S ENCLOSURE.

FIG. 37.—THE UNDERGROUND TEMPLE.

has been left unfinished. Had this been completed it would have had a lofty brick and plaster tower of the usual kind above it. Another temple built in the same manner, so far as the linga is concerned, is the small Śiva temple next to the monolithic statue of Narasimha, in which the base of the large stone linga still stands under water. A number of other cases of half-buried temples could be pointed out among the ruins, but until these are excavated it is not clear whether they were purposely constructed below the natural ground level or whether they have become nearly buried by the silt washed down upon them in the course of centuries from higher ground above. According to a stone inscription the Underground Temple was known as Prasanna Virūpāksha, i.e., the delighted Virūpāksha.

The road to Hampi now runs over a low rocky saddle, just missing a great chance of a striking effect by passing to one side of, instead of under, the wonderful natural arch made by the two gigantic rocks which lean against one another to the east of it [see Fig. 3]—and leads through one of the outer lines of walls of the city by a small ruined gateway. About half a mile further on, it turns sharply to the right between two small temples. The eastern of these is the temple of Uddāna Vīrabhadra, in which worship is still performed by the Lingāyats. Under the outer wall of it, on the edge of the road, stand two little sati stones and an inscription recording that the image inside the temple was set up in 1545. On the opposite side of the road, is the group of sati memorials illustrated in Fig. 11, and already described above.

A few yards further on the road crosses the Turuttu channel already mentioned.

Statue of Narasimha

A few yards to the west of the road at this point, standing in a walled enclosure, is a huge monolithic statue of Narasimha, the hideous Man-lion incarnation of Vishnu. An inscription on a stone slab set up in front of the enclosure records that it was hewn out of a single boulder by a Brāhman in 1528 * in the latter part of the reign of Krishna Dēva Rāya, who granted it an endowment. Although it is 22 feet high, the detail on it has been finished with great care and mutilated though

* *Epigraphia Indica*, I, 399.

it is, it still remains one of the most striking objects among the ruins. Originally, Narasimha's consort Lakshmi must have been portrayed sitting in the usual position on the thigh

FIG. 38.—MONOLITHIC STATUE OF NARASIMHA.

of the god, but the only part of her image that remains unbroken is the right arm she passed around his waist; the rest of it lies in shapeless fragments scattered about the enclosure. On the base of the pedestal is carved a representation of the sun and moon, denoting that the testimony of the statue will last for ever. The rubble masonry ramp abutting on to the walls inside the enclosure show that the latter was never completed. From the nature of its construction, it would appear that the original idea was to enshrine the image within a lofty temple but the building was left unfinished.

Large Stone Linga.

Alongside of the Narasimha statue is the small Śiva temple containing the enormous stone linga referred to above, the base of which stands permanently under water, and is illustrated in Fig. 10.

Krishna Temple.

On the rising ground immediately to the north of these two monuments is the large temple of Krishna, which is yet another of Krishna Dēva Rāya's additions to the city. An inscription within relates that he built it in 1513 (about the same time, that is, as the Throne Platform and Hazāra Rāma temple) to enshrine an image of Krishna* which he had captured, during his expedition against Orissa, from a temple in the hill-fortress of Udayagiri in the Nellore district. It is a large handsome temple containing the usual attendant shrines, mandapas and pillared verandahs around its court-yard and is provided with a granary on the south side which appears to be a later addition. The sculpture within the temple is not remarkable and calls for no remarks. The ruined gateways were originally crowned with the usual brick and plaster towers decorated with stucco figures. East of the temple, leading up to its main entrance, is one of the four ruined bazaars which are still standing. What was once the handsome street in which the temple car festival took place, is now a cultivated field.

Small Vishnu Temple.

Just beyond the Krishna temple and on the western side of the road are the two shrines illustrated in Fig. 40. The small plain stone-built shrine in the foreground contains a rather curious object of worship carved upon the natural sheet rock on which the little temple stands. This represents the footprints of Vishnu encircled by the serpent Sesha. In style, this little shrine resembles some of the small fourteenth century Jaina temples in South Kanara. The projecting ends of the stone beams carrying the roof and the board-like eaves

* This image is now in the Madras Museum.

FIG. 39.—KRISHNA TEMPLE.

FIG. 40.—SMALL VISHNU TEMPLE AND SĀSIVIKALLU GANĒSA MANDAPA.

indicate an unmistakable wooden origin for this style of building.

Sāsivikallu Ganēsa Statue.

This great monolithic image of the popular deity Ganēsa, the belly-god, which is ironically named the Sāsivikallu, or

FIG. 41.—SĀSIVIKALLU GANĒSA STATUE.

"the stone like a mustard seed" stands under the open pillared mandapa on the rocky hillock immediately above the little Vishnu shrine just described. The rat, the vahan or vehicle of Ganēsa, is carved on a separate piece of stone set up in front of the image.

Kadalaikallu Ganesa Temple.

A few yards further up the road one arrives at the top of the hill where the road descends somewhat suddenly to Hampi Bazaar below. On this saddle are situated a few ruined buildings of no particular interest and the handsome Kadalaikallu Ganēsa temple illustrated in Fig. 42. It contains a companion monolith of the same god which in the same spirit has been nicknamed the Kadalaikallu or the "grain-of-gram stone." The lofty pillars of the handsome hall in front of the sanctum which faces the east, and the noble doorway leading into the latter, together with the plain stone walls and flat roof-line, give the building a semi-classical appearance unlike any other building among the ruins. A very beautiful view of the country towards the north-east can be obtained from this temple, in which the picturesque Hampi Bazaar and the Tungabhadra beyond it, figure prominently. But one of the most striking views of all can be obtained by leaving the road by the former of these Ganēsa images and walking over the sheet rock to the north of it to the conspicuous two-storeyed mandapa which stands on the crest of the hill known as Hēmakutam. The Pampāpati temple with its picturesque towers lies below, beyond it the Tungabhadra, and beyond that again the rugged wilderness of hills in the Nizam's Dominions [see Fig. 43]. In the foreground stand a number of small stone temples belonging to a very early period and in all probability, they represent some of the earliest temples erected at Hampi. Some of them appear to have been originally Jaina temples which were subsequently converted into Hindu shrines. Hēmakutam is regarded as a very sacred spot and no doubt its sanctity goes back to a very early period.

Group of Jaina Temples.

Lower down the northern slope of the hill overlooking the courtyard of the Pampāpati temple is the largest group of Jaina-like temples in the city [see Fig. 44]. Their stepped pyramidal towers, so unlike anything else among the ruins are very noticeable. On plan, these temples are mostly cruciform and usually contain three shrine cells opening into a central pillared hall with a flight of steps in front which

FIG. 42.—KADALAIKALLU GANĒSA TEMPLE.

here faces the north. Although this style of architecture is usually referred to as Jaina, we often find Hindu temples built in the same style, but the Jains certainly favoured this style to a greater extent than the Hindus. Unlike the Hindus, the Jains almost invariably selected a picturesque site for the erection of their temples valuing rightly, the effect of environment on their architecture. Besides this group of temples in this style, there is the Gānigitti Jaina temple on the Kampli road which will be referred to later, two dilapidated examples to the east of the Elephant Stables, two more just north of the northern gopuram of the Pampāpati temple and yet another about a mile north-east of Hampi, standing on the hillside above the path which runs along the bank of the river to the Vitthala temple. So at one time the Jaina faith appears to have greatly flourished in these parts. The age of these shrines is uncertain, some of the smaller buildings on Hēmakutam Hill are undoubtedly the earliest. The simplicity of the style of some of these earlier examples recall in outline the Pallava temples of the seventh century and it is possible that a few of them may date back to that early period. The larger and more ornate temples with the stepped towers are obviously later, and, in all probability, these are not earlier than the fourteenth or fifteenth century.

The Pampāpati Temple.

On leaving these temples and passing through the ruined gateway on the east, which affords access to them from the path above, the visitor passes down a steep path leading over the rocks into Hampi Bazaar below and arrives outside the main entrance into the enclosure surrounding the temple of Pampāpati or Virūpāksha, the oldest and most sacred Hindu temple in the city. The meaning of the word Pampā, and the original characteristics of Siva in the form of Virūpāksha, have already been explained in *Part I.* The main shrine contains a stone linga of the usual kind which is worshipped as the symbol of Pampā, or Virūpāksha. Parts of the temple, as already mentioned, are older than the founding of the kingdom of Vijayanagar itself. Later additions were of course made and Harihara I, the first of the Vijayanagar rulers, is credited with having built a temple here in honour of Mādhava or Vidyāranya, the Brāhman sage who had helped him in the founding of the city, and as an inscription within

FIG. 43.—NORTH VIEW FROM HĒMAKUTAM HILL.

it shows Krishna Dēva Rāya built (in 1509-10) the ranga-mandapa in front of the god's shrine in honour of his coronation. He is also credited with having constructed the big eastern and northern gateways, but another account states that the latter is called the Kannagiri Gopuram and was built by a chief of the place of that name in the Nizam's Dominions. It was repaired in 1837, when temples were still under the management of Government, by Mr. F. W. Robertson, the then Collector of the district, and is decorated in an unusual style with many clusters of little pilasters and very few of the stucco figures with which these buildings are usually so profusely decorated.

The shrine to Bhuvanēsvari contains a beautifully executed Chālukyan doorway flanked by the pierced stone windows characteristic of the style, and several Chālukyan pillars carved in black stone. Work of this style belongs to the eleventh or twelfth century and, therefore, this shrine must have been in existence prior to the founding of the kingdom of Vijayanagar. The Portuguese traveller Paes visited the Pampāpati temple in the reign of Krishna Rāya and from his description published in Mr. Sewell's "Forgotten Empire," the temple seems to have presented much the same appearance then as it does now. He states:—"In this pagoda, opposite to its principal gate which is to the east, there is a very beautiful street of very beautiful houses with balconies and arcades, in which are sheltered the pilgrims that come to it, and there are also houses for the lodging of the upper classes; the King has a palace in the same street, in which he resides when he visits this pagoda. There is a (representation) of a pomegranate tree * above this first gate; the gate has a very lofty tower all covered with rows of men and women and hunting scenes and many other representations, and as the tower goes narrowing towards the top so the images diminish in size. Passing this first gate, you come at once into a large courtyard with another gate of the same sort as the first, except that it is rather smaller throughout; and passing this second gate, there is a large court with

* Paes here refers to the stucco representation of Krishna in the Tree and the gopis below begging for their clothes.

FIG. 44.—GROUP OF JAINA TEMPLES, SOUTH OF THE PAMPĀPATI TEMPLE.

verandahs all round on pillars of stone, and in the middle of this court is the house of the idol.

Opposite the principal gate stand four columns (stambhas), two gilded and the other two copper, for all are of copper. That which stands nearest the gate of the temple was given by this King Crisnarāo (Krishna Rāya) who now reigns here, and the others by his predecessors. All the outer side of the gate of the temple (doorway of the main shrine) up to the roof is covered with copper and gilded, and on each side of the roof on the top are certain great animals that look like tigers, all gilt. As soon as you enter this idol shrine, you perceive from pillar to pillar on which it is supported many little holes in which stand oil lamps, which burn, so they tell me, every night, and they will be in number, two thousand five hundred or three thousand lights. As soon as you pass this shrine, you enter another small one like the crypt of some church; it has two doors at the sides, and thence onward this building is like a chapel, where stands the idol which they adore. Before you get to it there are three doors; the shrine is vaulted and dark without any light from the sky; it is always lit with candles (lamps). At the first gate are door-keepers who never allow any one to enter except the Brāhmans that have charge of it, and I, because I gave something to them, was allowed to enter.

Between gate and gate are images of little idols. The principal idol is a round stone (linga) without any shape; they have great devotion for it. This building outside is all covered with copper gilt. At the back of the temple outside, close to the verandahs of which I have spoken, there is a small idol of white alabaster with six arms, in one it has a sword, and in the others sacred emblems, and it has below its feet a buffalo, and a large animal which is helping to kill that buffalo.* In this pagoda there burns continually a lamp of ghee (oil) and around are other small temples for houses of devotion.

The other temples aforesaid are made in the same manner, but this one is the principal one and the oldest; they all

* This refers to an image of the goddess Durga killing the buffalo demon. A very popular goddess.

FIG. 45.—HAMPI BAZAAR FROM THE EAST.

have many buildings and gardens with many trees, in which the Brāhmans cultivate their vegetables, and other herbs that they eat. Whenever the festival of any of these temples occurs they drag along certain triumphal cars which run on wheels, and with it go dancing-girls and other women with music to the temple (conducting) the idol along the said street with much pomp."

Hampi Bazaar.

Standing outside the temple are two wooden cars but neither are very old, in fact one was made only two or three years ago, but it is interesting to think that the car festival referred to by Paes continues at the present day. During the big annual festival in the spring, every house and shelter in this old bazaar is occupied by a crowd of some twenty thousand people who come from all parts of the Madras Presidency and the Nizam's Dominions and collect round about the Pampāpati temple at this period and remain there for about ten days. The car is dragged from the eastern gateway of the temple to the two-storeyed building at the other end of the street and thence back to the temple. It is an interesting sight to watch this performance taking place and to see the old bazaar once again filled with shops and booths, and a vast and happy crowd enjoying itself. But for this annual festival, this street would, in all probability, be under cultivation like the others. It is about 35 yards wide and 800 yards in length, and is the finest of the four which still stand. At its eastern end is a large but clumsily executed Nandi, or sacred bull of Siva which faces the temple. It is shaped out of a natural boulder and stands under a dilapidated mandapa behind the two-storeyed building with the polished Chālukyan pillars already referred to. The buildings in this street belong to the temple authorities and the amount of rent they collect every year from the better class pilgrims who occupy the houses must be considerable.

BUILDINGS ON THE NORTHERN AND EASTERN SIDES OF THE CITY.

Kōdanda Rāma Temple.

At the eastern end of Hampi Bazaar a path leads over the rocks to the Soolai Bazaar and Achyuta Rāya's temple, but a pleasanter and more interesting way of getting there, is to take the stone-paved pathway near this end of the street

FIG. 46.—MONOLITHIC BULL AT THE EASTERN END OF HAMPI BAZAAR.

which leads towards the river and thereafter winds among the huge rocks on its brink to the temple of Kōdanda Rāma, which lies just opposite to the gorge which has been referred to above. During the floods the sight the river presents at this spot is most impressive. The whole body of the stream is hurled through a narrow channel the depth of which must be considerable. The force of the stream is strongly exhibited in the large cavities worn in the rocks which become visible when the river is low. The temple in which regular worship is still performed is regarded as an important place of pilgrimage and faces the most sacred bathing-pool in the river but is itself of no architectural interest and has been spoilt by modern additions.

Soolai Bazaar.

Keeping still to the river bank and proceeding in a north-easterly direction, one arrives at the northern end of another large street in ruins. This is known as the Soolai Bazaar, or Dancing-girls' Street and leads up to Achyuta Rāya's temple. The dancing-girls are said to have occupied this street in which also the annual car festival of the temple was held. The houses are in ruins and the street is under cultivation but sufficient remains to show that it was once a handsome thoroughfare. The sacred Matanga Parvatam behind gives the temple and the street a very picturesque setting. Near the north-western end of the street is a tank or bath with a ruined pavilion in its centre which we may presume was used by the dancing-girls. Originally rubble walls plastered over, separated the quarters for each dancing-girl, in the same manner as may still be seen in some of the ruined houses in Hampi Bazaar. It is a curious fact that, although the temples, palaces and civil buildings were built on such a lavish scale, the domestic dwellings and private houses must have been of the poorest description as no trace of them other than the ruined car streets survive. It is unlikely that the Muhammadans would have troubled themselves about wrecking these when there were so many more valuable buildings to destroy. In all probability, the dwellings of the humbler classes were even more squalid and ill-arranged than they are in any big city in India at the present day. The glowing accounts of the "beautiful streets with very beautiful houses with balconies and arcades" which the old chroniclers have furnished us with, relate almost exclusively to the few car streets of the larger temples. One would imagine that even these descriptions were rather overdrawn judging from

FIG. 47.—THE TUNGABHADRA IN FLOOD.

Fig. 48.—The Dancing-girls' Bath in the Soolai Bazaar.

FIG. 49.—ACHYUTA RĀYA'S TEMPLE.

the style of the houses that still remain in Hampi Bazaar which is said to have been the finest street in the city.

The Achyuta Rāya's Temple.

This is another of the larger temples and is situated in a double walled enclosure of great size with lofty gateways, an Amman shrine, and numerous mandapas and verandahs in various stages of decay. The temple has the usual pillared hall in front, now in ruins, and faces the north. Inscriptions on its gateways show that it was built by King Achyuta Rāya in 1539. It is designed on similar lines to the famous Vitthala temple but will not bear comparison with that superb building. However, it contains some handsome pillars and carefully finished sculpture. The cloister-like verandah running all round the inner courtyard with its carved pillars and small engaged columns and handsome plinth, decorated with well-carved panels representing an elephant procession, is a handsome piece of work as may be seen in Fig. 50. The carving here is excellent considering it is executed in granite. The best work will be found in the panels between the plinth and cornice mouldings of the basement on the west and north-western sides of the verandah. Here, near the gateway on the west, will be found the curious bas-relief representing a combination of a bull and an elephant shown in Fig. 51. The stone-carving of the ruined gateways, too, deserves notice, particularly that on the northern gateway of the inner courtyard illustrated in Fig. 52. The stone work of this is decorated with the different incarnations and the conch and chakram symbols of Vishnu, with little figures of Krishna here and there. The bases of the inner and outer doorjambs contain graceful female figures, one on either side, representing in duplicate, the river goddess Gangā or the Ganges, standing on the back of a makara or conventional crocodile from the mouth of which issues a floriated scroll ornament of semi-classical character which is continued all round the door-frame and forms a very pleasing ornament. This particular design of two river goddesses acting as the guardians to the temple and the floriated ornament is a common feature in the temples of Northern and Central India, but there, the female figures always represent the Ganges and the Jumna respectively, the latter goddess being represented as standing on the back of a tortoise. There is little doubt

FIG. 50.—VERANDAH IN THE INNER COURTYARD OF ACHYUTA RĀYA'S TEMPLE.

that this design originated in Northern India where it sometimes occurs in Hindu temples of about the eighth century.

Fig. 51.—Verandah in the inner courtyard of Achyuta Rāya's Temple, detail of a carved panel.

The goddess Yamuna, or the Jumna, is not met with south of the Ganjām district, from thence southwards, her place is taken by a duplicate figure of Gangā. Very few of the Brāhman priests in Southern India, appear to know what these two female figures represent, and like the lower

FIG. 52.—NORTHERN GATEWAY OF THE INNER COURTYARD OF ACHYUTA RĀYA'S TEMPLE.

classes, appear to imagine that they have been specially executed, like the obscene sculpture one sometimes sees on temples and cars, to "avert the evil eye." The beautiful floriated scroll ornament issuing from the monster's mouth too, is obviously a design which has come from Northern India, and is probably mainly Greek in origin.

In the north-western corner of the outer courtyard, is a large and nicely carved Kalyāna Mandapa, or hall in which the annual marriage ceremony of the god and goddess took place. During this ceremony the images were placed on the raised platform at the back of the hall.

Matanga Parvatam.

The visitor who desires to climb to the top of the sacred hill known as Matanga Parvatam, referred to above, should pass through the little gateway to the south of the temple and follow the water channel to the west until he arrives at the flight of stone steps which leads up the hill on this side to the temple on its summit. The temple contains a black stone image of Vishnu in the form of Parasu Rāma in duplicate, a female figure representing the god's consort, and three stone bulls. The shrine is built of stone pillars with rubble masonry walls in between supporting a flat stone roof crowned with a brick and plaster tower, or 'stūpi' as it is called in Southern India, of the usual kind. There are several little attendant shrines, now empty, and halls or mandapas attached to the main shrine. The stone pillars and the board-like eaves are of an early pattern, probably about the fourteenth century. The entrance doorway into the shrine contains some excellent stucco ornament that has been spoilt by multitudinous coats of whitewash. There are two little pilasters on either side of the doorway with double bracket capitals of Indo-Corinthian appearance, the acanthus leaf being unmistakable. One capital contains two little human figures in the form of atlantes supporting the abacus above. There is also a little string course, connecting two of the pilasters, decorated with a row of sacred geese, a favourite design of the Buddhists. To the archæologist, the temple is interesting but as an architectural monument, it is unworthy of notice. However, the superb view of the city, the river, and the surrounding country will well repay the visitor for the trouble of climbing the hill. I do not think there is a more interesting or beautiful view than this, in the whole of Southern India. Although the ascent up the hill looks a rather formidable undertaking from below, it is in reality an easy climb to the top as the steps are in good order. So far as one's comfort is concerned, the best time to ascend the hill is in the early morning, as in the evening, the heat given off from the rocks is rather trying unless there should happen to be a breeze blowing. Whether morning or evening the view is equally wonderful and charming.

The Varaha Temple.

As there are no ruins of interest on the southern side of Achyuta Rāya's temple, the visitor should retrace his steps to the footpath that runs along the northern end of the Soolai Bazaar. At this end of the street, on the opposite side of the path, is a ruined temple and a large unfinished gateway leading into the same. Carved on the inner walls of this gateway, may be observed the Varāha, or boar incarnation of Vishnu, standing before a drawn sword with the sun and moon represented above the figure [see Fig. 5]. This device was used by the rulers of Vijayanagar as their crest and occurs on several monuments set up during that period. The building is known, locally, as the Varāha Perumal temple. To the west of this standing at the extreme north-western end of the Soolai Bazaar surrounded by jungle growth, is a picturesque little ruin representing another Vaishnava shrine dedicated to Anantasayana or Vishnu reclining on the coils of the serpent Sēsha, illustrating the birth of Brahma. A ruined stucco representation of the scene is depicted above the cornice of the front of the building.

Anantasayana Shrines.

On the eastern side of the northern end of the Soolai Bazaar, standing on a raised masonry platform immediately above the pathway leading to the Vitthala temple, is another little temple of Vishnu containing a similar representation of Anantasayana carved upon a natural boulder over which the temple has been built. This sculpture is well preserved and nicely carved and is worthy of notice. It is situated about 40 yards to the east of the Varāha temple. One of the best bas-reliefs among the ruins portraying Anantasayana is the one illustrated in Fig. 53. It is carved upon a natural rock situated on the brink of the river to the north-east of the Varāha temple and is under water during high flood. Another good example of the same scene, but unfortunately mutilated, is the one on the verandah of the Traveller's Rest-house at Kāmalāpur. One of the largest and loftiest shrines ever set up at Hampi, is the Anantasayana temple at

Fig. 53.—Rock-cut Image of Anantasayana, illustrating the birth of Brahma.

Anantasainagudi, a village one mile from Hospet on the road to Kāmalāpur which will be referred to later.

Jaina Temple near the river.

After passing the Anantasayana temple to the east of the Soolai Bazaar and the few ruined shrines near it, which are unimportant and call for no remarks, the path leads on to the Jaina-like temple illustrated in Fig. 54. It stands on rising ground above the pathway facing the river and has the usual stepped tower over the shrine which is generally associated with Jaina temples. The shrine itself faces the east and has the usual pillared hall in front and is surrounded by a walled enclosure. It has a two-storeyed mandapa on the south and is provided by a flight of stone steps leading up to the court-yard on its northern side. Outside, is the usual stambha or stone-pillar. The shrine contains no idol, and the bas-relief sculptures are all Vaishnava in character. Thus Lakshmi, the consort of Vishnu, occupies the place of honour over the doorways into the hall in front of the shrine, and figures of Hanumān and Garuda respectively are carved on each side of both doorways, while on the bases of the southern entrance are two representations of Vishnu acting as the door-keeper or guardian of the temple. On the side walls of the entrance passage into the sanctum, outside, is the figure of an elephant, similar to the one carved on the sati stone standing in front of the temple near the path referred to above. These Vaishnava sculptures would lead one to suppose that it is not a Jaina temple, in spite of the fact that it is built in the particular style which they usually adopted. However, as in South Kanara, Jaina temples are often covered in Hindu figures, in fact built by Hindu masons, and when asked why they permit their temples to be decorated with representations of the great Hindu deities, the Jain usually replies that these figures merely show that the Hindu gods are subordinate to the Jaina saint or 'tirthankara' inshrined in the sanctum. The fact that a four-armed figure of Vishnu is represented here as the door-keeper of this temple may indicate that it really is a Jaina temple in spite of the other Vaishnava sculptures. In cases of this kind, the only true test is the character of the idol inshrined in the sanctum, but, unfortunately, the sanctum in this instance is empty. As a rule, the cross-legged, seated, nude figure representing one of the

FIG. 54.—JAINA TEMPLE ON A HILLOCK FACING THE RIVER.

twenty-four Jinas or saints, that one usually finds in a Jaina temple, bears a distinctive sign, such as a bull, elephant, monkey, crocodile, or lion carved upon the base of the idol or on its pedestal. It is possible that the figure of the elephant carved upon the outer walls of the passage leading into the cella may have been represented here for this purpose denoting the particular Jaina saint to whom the temple was originally dedicated. Otherwise, its position on the temple is difficult to account for as it does not appear to be a mere ornament and the 'elephant' has no special significance in the cult of Vishnu. The Jains had no particular architectural style of their own, although they certainly favoured the stepped pyramidal tower, a cruciform plan, and had monolithic pillars or stambhas in front of their shrines. But then, so did the Hindus, so, as far as mere style is concerned, these things in themselves are not a safe guide, and unless the figure of a Jaina saint is carved on the dedicatory block on the lintel over the shrine doorway, or there is a Jaina image in the sanctum, one cannot be certain as to whether temples built in this particular style are Jaina or Hindu. The group of temples on Hĕmakutam, for instance, are always referred to as the 'Jaina temples' but we have no real evidence to show that they were set up by the Jains and many of them are undoubtedly Siva temples.

Sugriva's Cave. Opposite to this temple, facing the path is the cave (conspicuously marked with the usual red and white vertical lines) in which Sugriva kept Sita's jewels, and the mark on the rock made by her garment as it fell. **The old bridge.** Beyond it are the remains of a ruined bridge which crossed the river on monolithic pillars. Judging from the remains, it appears to have been originally constructed on the same lines as those employed in building the car streets and temple verandahs, namely, two rows of monolithic uprights carrying cross beams supporting flat roof slabs. Advantage was taken of the small islands and the shallowness of the river at this point but even then, it was a rather daring undertaking and it is unlikely that it could have stood for very long if it was ever completed which seems doubtful, as none of the early visitors mention it. Paes (1520) says the people always crossed in round basket boats covered with leather, a type of boat which is still in use on the Tungabhadra at the present day. So if it was ever finished, it must have been after his visit. A view of what remains of it is given in Fig. 55.

The path now leads past a number of small ruined shrines under a lofty two-storeyed gateway and up to and under, the curious monument illustrated in Fig. 13. This is the King's

King's Balance.

Balance, or more correctly the Tulāpurusha-dāna monument mentioned above. Proceeding forward, the path passes through the remains of a large unfinished gateway up to the enclosure of the famous Vitthala temple. The monolithic pillars forming the jambs of this great gateway are beautifully decorated with figures of Gangā and floriated scroll ornament similar to that which we noticed on the gateways of Achyuta Rāya's temple. To the north of it, is a small but well built little temple of Vishnu, of excellent proportion and designed in good taste and picturesquely situated. It contains no idol and the tower over its shrine is in ruins but it is, nevertheless, an interesting little building worthy of notice. It contains inscriptions which relate that it was built by Sadasiva Rāya in A.D. 1561–1562.

The Vitthala Temple.

We now pass on to the Vitthala temple, the most splendid building in the city. It was dedicated to Vishnu in the form of Vitthala or Vithōba. Vithōba is a god of the Maratha country and is rarely met with outside it. He is regarded as a form of Krishna. In and about the temple are no less than 23 inscriptions of dates ranging from A.D. 1513 to 1564. Several of these are damaged, but those which are still legible show that Krishna Dēva Rāya, to whom the city owes so much began the temple in 1513 and endowed it with villages; that his two queens built the gateways and presented golden vessels to the shrine; and that his two successors Achyuta and Sadāsiva, and many private individuals, made gifts of various kinds to the building. The temple was never finished nor consecrated. In all probability, the work was stopped by the destruction of the city in 1565, but tradition gives another reason and says that it was built specially for the famous image of Vithōba at Pandharpur in the Sholāpur district of Bombay but that the god, having come to look at it, refused to move, saying that it was too grand for him and that he preferred his own humbler home.

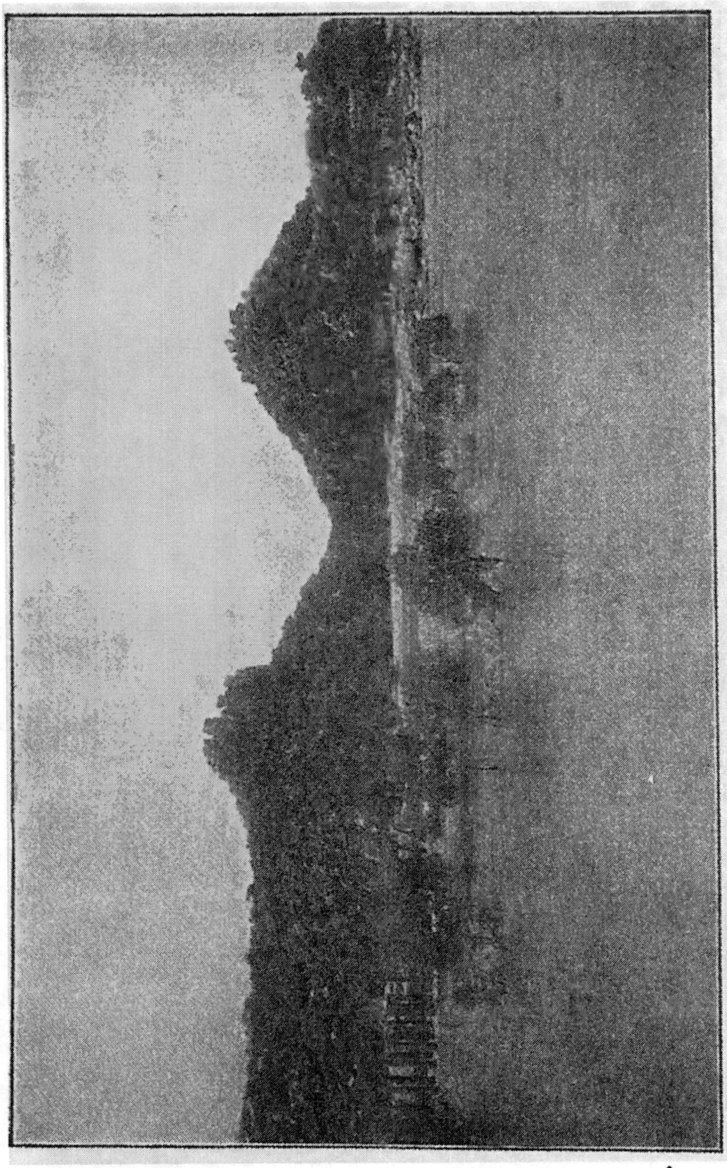

FIG. 55.—THE RUINED BRIDGE.

FIG. 56.—VITTHALA TEMPLE.

The temple stands in a high walled, stone-paved enclosure with three gateways on the north, south and east sides, respectively. All of them are now in ruins and the larger one on the eastern side was found to be in such a dangerous

FIG. 57.—VITTHALA TEMPLE, NORTH ENTRANCE INTO MAIN SHRINE.

condition that it had to be closed to the public. The temple has the usual Amman shrine, attendant temples and mandapas and cloister-like verandahs running round the courtyard. The flat-roof over the shrine is ornamented with a brick and plaster dome-shaped stūpı of the usual type and there was, originally, an ornamental brick and plaster parapet wall decorated with little niches filled with stucco figures above

FIG. 58.—VITTHALA TEMPLE, INTERIOR VIEW.

the cornice of the large pillared hall with side porches which adorns the front or eastern side of the shrine. In spite of the fact that the roof over this magnificent hall was never completed and that many of its beautiful pillars have been grievously damaged by the destroyers of the city, it is still the finest building of its kind in Southern India, and to

FIG. 59.—VITTHALA TEMPLE, DETAILS OF PLINTH AND CORNICE.

quote Fergusson—"shows the extreme limit in florid magnificence to which the style advanced." The building stands on a richly carved basement, decorated with a procession of the king's horses, conventional geese, and some exquisite mouldings, including the beautiful bracelet moulding similar to that which we noticed at the Hazāra Rāma temple. The steps leading up to the front of the hall are flanked by two large stone elephants which are sadly mutilated. Perhaps, the most wonderful feature of the whole building is the style of the elaborate composite pillars with clusters of little free-standing columns and conventional animals with little riders on their backs, attached to them in front, each pillar being carved out of a single block of granite. The bases and bracket capitals are equally richly carved with beautiful mouldings and little bas-relief figures. The hall is cruciform on plan, the four side halls or porches leading into one large central hall, now roofless. Around each hall above the mighty cross beams carrying the roof slabs is a beautifully sculptured frieze, representing, in bas-relief, scenes from the Rāmāyana. The carved ceilings too are very beautiful and the size of the stone beams and slabs used in their construction is most remarkable. A very striking feature of the building is the beauty of its curved stone eaves, or dripstones as they are usually called. A glance at their underside shows clearly enough that these were copied from a wooden model, the outer surface of which was covered with thin metal plates decorated with embossed brass or copper gilt ornaments with rings at the angles for the hanging of lamps or bells, all of which features are reproduced here in stone, in the same manner as we noticed in the eaves adorning the Hazāra Rāma temple. Both temples were started in the same year, and judging from their style, it would appear that they were decorated by the same sculptors so far as details of this kind are concerned. It was not an uncommon practice at this period, for an important shrine to be covered outside from top to bottom with copper gilt plates and embossed ornaments. The main shrine of the Pampāpati temple for instance was decorated in this manner when Paes visited it as may be gathered from his description cited above. Until quite recently, the famous Śiva temple at Srisailam in the Kurnool district was covered with copper gilt plates, and ornaments some of which may now be seen in the Madras Museum. When these great temples were finished, they were always whitewashed from roof to plinth, the main features of the building being picked out in gaudy colours. A good example of this will be found in the magnificent Kalyāna Mandapa standing in the courtyard to the south-east of the Vitthala

FIG. 60.—VITTHALA TEMPLE, STONE CAR.

temple, in which some of the original old colour work still remains. The ceilings too were usually painted, in fact the entire building, inside and out and from top to bottom, was decorated in this manner. The only portion of the temples that appear to have escaped this treatment are the interiors of the shrine chambers. These mighty shrines, as the inscriptions sometimes inform us, were set up with a view to their "lasting for ever," with the result that many forms which would ordinarily have been executed in wood protected by a metal covering were reproduced in stone with this object in view.

In any other temple, the beauty of the Kalyāna Mandapa alone would be sufficient to excite wonder and admiration in its beholder. It is a magnificent building and built on similar lines to the mahāmandapa or great hall in front of the main shrine and contains a daïs in its centre for the reception of the images of the god and goddess during their annual marriage ceremony. In front of the main temple is the stone car of the god. It is a very handsome little stone built structure which was originally crowned with a small brick and plaster dome-shaped stūpi similar to that over the main shrine. Some writers have asserted that it is carved out of a single block of stone, but such is not the case. The joints between the masonry are so beautifully fine that any one might easily be led to believe that it is monolithic. Pilgrims believe that religious merit may be obtained by turning round its stone wheels, with the result that the axles, which are also of stone, have been worn away to an alarming degree. Two elephants guard the entrance to the car which is approached by a very wooden-like stone ladder.

The Amman shrine, and the few other attendant buildings in the courtyard, which in any other situation would be considered notable instances of patient, careful workmanship are entirely dwarfed by the magnificence of the great hall and the Kalyāna Mandapa just described. In the mandapa on the southern side of the courtyard is a collection of broken sculptures discovered when the enclosure was cleared of rubbish and jungle growth. The sculptures are broken and mutilated but some of them still exhibit signs of excellent workmanship.

Facing the eastern gateway of the temple are the remains of another ruined car street or bazaar and a small Śiva temple to the north of it. On the south side, there is also another temple and a ruined mandapa of no particular interest. The path follows the ruined bazaar to the east and eventually joins the main road between Kāmalāpur and Talarigattu [see the Map].

FIG. 61.—VITTHALA TEMPLE, KALYĀNA MANDAPA.

Mālyavānta Raghunātha Temple.

Returning to Kāmalāpur by the Talarigattu road, one passes a large tank and the Mālyavanta Raghunātha temple beyond it which is situated on the commanding hill to the east of the road [see the Map]. The entrance, however, is on the

FIG. 62.—VITTHALA TEMPLE, KALYĀNA MANDAPA, INTERIOR VIEW.

Kampli road. The temple stands in a high-walled enclosure and has the usual gateways and attendant buildings. The main object of worship, here, is a figure of Rāma carved upon a huge boulder and the stūpi of the shrine is perched on the

FIG. 63.—MĀLYAVANTA RAGHUNĀTHA TEMPLE, SOUTHERN ENTRANCE.

top of this as may be seen in Fig. 64. The large hall in front of the temple and the Kalyāna Mandapa contain the best

FIG.—64. MĀLYAVANTA RAGHUNĀTHA TEMPLE, GENERAL VIEW FROM THE EAST.

sculpture and workmanship. The quaint fishes, marine monsters and serpents carved on the walls of the courtyard deserve notice. Among these, may be observed two serpents approaching the sun (or moon) representing a solar or lunar eclipse. On the top of the hill is the rather striking cleft in the rock shown in Fig. 65. It is said to be the work of Rāma's arrow and is one of the chief attractions to the pilgrims who

FIG. 65.—MĀLYAVANTA RAGHUNĀTHA TEMPLE, CLEFT IN THE ROCK.

visit this temple. On each side of the fissure, carved on the natural rock, are a number of lingas and sacred bulls. Above it, perched on a boulder, is a little brick and a plaster Śiva shrine. For many years this large temple was empty and deserted, but a few years ago a *bairāgi* from Behar settled down in it, revived the worship, and organized a car festival. The temple is the property of the Government and only leased to the *bairāgi* on certain conditions. It is not a particularly

Fig. 66.—Gānigitti Jaina Temple.

interesting monument, and unless the visitor has plenty of time to spare it is hardly worth a visit, but it is a place of importance to the pious pilgrim.

Gānigitti Jaina Temple.

Further along the road, about half a mile from the Kāmalāpur Resthouse, on the southern side of the road, is the

FIG. 67.—PATTĀBHI RĀMA TEMPLE.

Gānigitti temple. Gānigitti means 'an oil-woman' and why the temple should be so named is not apparent. It is a Jaina temple and the tower above its shrine is built in the series of steps which is the most noticeable feature of this style. The handsome monolithic stambha or pillar in front of the entrance bears an important inscription from which we learn that the temple was erected by a Jaina general named Irugapa in 1385, during the reign of Harihara II, who must have been a king who was tolerant in religious matters. Even without the help of the inscription, there is no difficulty in this case, in ascertaining its Jaina origin, for over the front door way is carved upon the stone lintel a small seated figure of a Jaina saint, with three superimposed umbrellas above its head and a fly-whisk on either side. Again, above the flat roof over the front porch is an ornamental brick and plaster parapet containing three large niches containing in crumbling plaster, the remains of three seated Jaina images of the same saint as that which appears on the door lintel. It is a carefully built temple and free from Hindu sculpture and is quite the most valuable Jaina monument among the ruins.

Chandrasēkara Temple. Almost opposite to this temple, at a short distance from the road, is the Siva shrine known as the Chandrasēkara temple. It is situated close to the Queen's Bath and is one of the first monuments the visitor meets with when going in that direction. It is of no particular artistic or historic interest but is a well built compact little building.

Pattābhi Rāma Temple. This is the largest temple among the ruins and is situated half a mile to the east of Kāmalāpur on the road to Bellary. An inscription within shows that it was built by Achyuta Rāya (A.D. 1530–1542), and is remarkable for little but its size and the lofty proportions of its great hall in front of the shrine which faces the east. It is, however, a fine structure and deserves notice. To appreciate buildings of this class at their true value, one should visit them before seeing such magnificent buildings as the Vitthala and Hazāra Rāma temples, for the former are entirely dwarfed by the magnificence of the latter and in comparison appear commonplace.

The Anantasayana Temple near Hospet. The only other building of importance that has not yet been described, is the great temple of Anantasayana at Anantasainagudi, a village one mile from Hospet on the road

FIG. 68.—ANANTASAYANA TEMPLE NEAR HOSPET.

to Kāmalāpur. A description of this curious temple has been reserved for the last as the visitor will find it convenient to see it on his way back to Hospet. The inner shrine of this great building is oblong on plan and contains a correspondingly lengthy pedestal for the accommodation of the huge image of Anantasayana for which it was originally built. But the most wonderful part of the whole building is its roof. This takes the form of a long barrel vaulted roof with rounded apse-like ends constructed in brick and is a marvel of engineering skill. The front of the building is provided with a handsome pillared hall with a flat roof of the usual type and faces the north and is completely spoilt by its squalid surroundings. There are no inscriptions to inform us of the name of the King who built it, but being so close to Nāgalāpur (Hospet) we may presume that it represents yet another of Krishna Rāya's wonderful works. The plan of the building is not an uncommon one for temples built in honour of Anantasayana, as images of Vishnu in this particular form, where the god is always represented as lying, full length upon the folds of Sēsha in the manner shown in Fig. 53, must necessarily require a building that is oblong on plan, as it would not be possible to house a large image of this kind in a small square cella of the usual type as the length of the image is so very much greater than its breadth. The large image for which the temple was built now lies at Holalu in the south-western corner of the Hadagalli taluk of the district. It is carved in black stone with a power and finish quite out of the ordinary and is a beautiful piece of workmanship. It was apparently executed elsewhere and brought to Holalu, as no stone of the kind of which it is made is procurable locally. The popular legend connecting it with the temple at Anantasainagudi is that, when the idol was completed, a man was sent to conduct it to its new home. The god agreed to come on the condition that his guide went in front and did not look back during the journey. As usually happens in such stories, the man broke the agreement to see if the god was really following and the image has in consequence remained immovable at Holalu ever since. It is an old story and the truth perhaps is that internal commotions at Vijayanagar or external dangers to the empire prevented the project from ever being carried out.

FIG. 69.—MUHAMMADAN TOMBS AT KADIRÂMPURAM.

At a distance of 4½ miles from Hospet there is a branch road leading off the Kāmalāpur road to the village of Kadirāmpuram to the north and thence on to Hampi [see the Map]. By the side of this road, at the distance of nearly a mile from its junction with the Hospet road, may be seen the only Muhammadan tombs of any interest in this neighbourhood. These consist of a large walled enclosure containing three small tombs and a small domed structure standing near it in the remains of an extensive Muhammadan cemetery. Nothing is known concerning their history but from the size of the larger building, we may assume that some important personages were buried here. This enclosure wall is faced with well dressed stone, both within and without, and is relieved with arched openings all round and is a handsome structure. The smaller domed tomb is of the usual type and calls for no special remarks.

Muhammadan Tombs.

And here we may take leave of Hampi ruins. If the traveller visits all the various buildings referred to above, he may safely return to Hospet feeling that he has seen all the remains of this wonderful old city which are deserving of notice. With the exception of the Pampāpati temple, Hampi Bazaar, and the Kodanda Rāma temple, all the ruins belong to Government and the visitor may enter any portion of the buildings and go wherever he pleases. Name boards have been provided to all the monuments worthy of notice, and signposts will shortly be set up at the junctions of all roads throughout the ruins. So, with this assistance and the aid of the Map given here, the visitor should have no trouble in finding his way about the ruins without the assistance of a local guide.